Dark Psychology

What You Need to Know About Persuasion, Manipulation, NLP, Negotiation, Deception, and Human Psychology

© Copyright 2020

All Rights Reserved. No part of this book may be reproduced in any form without permission in writing from the author. Reviewers may quote brief passages in reviews.

Disclaimer: No part of this publication may be reproduced or transmitted in any form or by any means, mechanical or electronic, including photocopying or recording, or by any information storage and retrieval system, or transmitted by email without permission in writing from the publisher.

While all attempts have been made to verify the information provided in this publication, neither the author nor the publisher assumes any responsibility for errors, omissions or contrary interpretations of the subject matter herein.

This book is for entertainment purposes only. The views expressed are those of the author alone, and should not be taken as expert instruction or commands. The reader is responsible for his or her own actions.

Adherence to all applicable laws and regulations, including international, federal, state and local laws governing professional licensing, business practices, advertising and all other aspects of doing business in the US, Canada, UK or any other jurisdiction is the sole responsibility of the purchaser or reader.

Neither the author nor the publisher assumes any responsibility or liability whatsoever on the behalf of the purchaser or reader of these materials. Any perceived slight of any individual or organization is purely unintentional.

Contents

SECTION 1: DARK PSYCHOLOGY 1

INTRODUCTION 2

PART 1: THE DARK SIDE 4

CHAPTER 1: DARK PSYCHOLOGY: THE DARK TRIAD 5

    ABOUT THE DARK TRIAD 5

    HOW TO IDENTIFY DARK TRIAD TRAITS 6

    MANAGING PEOPLE WITH DARK TRIAD TRAITS 7

    HOW TO COPE WITH ANGER 7

    HOW TO DEAL WITH BULLYING 8

    SPOTTING A MANIPULATOR 8

    DEALING WITH NARCISSISM 9

    BUILDING THE SKILLS THAT YOU MAY NEED TO COPE 10

    THE IMPACT OF THE DARK TRIAD AT THE WORKPLACE 10

    GUARDING YOURSELF AGAINST THE UNDUE INFLUENCE OF DARK TRIAD INDIVIDUALS 11

CHAPTER 2: THE NINE DARK PERSONALITY TRAITS 14

CHAPTER 3: DARK CRIMINALS AMONG US 17

CRIMINAL MIND VS. CYBERCRIMINAL MIND 19
THE ROLE OF PSYCHOLOGY IN THE LEGAL SYSTEM 19
THE ROLES OF A CRIMINAL PSYCHOLOGIST.. 20
PROFILING... 21
APPLIED CRIMINAL PSYCHOLOGY 23

CHAPTER 4: QUIZ: ARE YOU A DARK PERSONALITY? 24
INTRODUCTION 24

PART 2: MIND CONTROL, DECEPTION, AND MANIPULATION 28

CHAPTER 5: CREEPY FACTS ABOUT MIND CONTROL 29
DAILY MIND CONTROL 32
MK-ULTRA... 33
ABOUT LSD 34

CHAPTER 6: DECEPTION DETECTION: HOW TO IDENTIFY A LIE .. 36
DETECTING DECEPTION 36
HOW TO DETECT AN ANOMALY 36
SIGNS OF DECEPTION 37

CHAPTER 7: WHAT MAKES A CULT? 10 BRAINWASHING TELL-TALE SIGNS.. 40
DISINTEGRATING THE CULT PSYCHOLOGY 40

CHAPTER 8: MEDIA MANIPULATION: STRATEGIES AND HOW TO SEE THROUGH THEM 47
MEDIA MANIPULATION... 47

CHAPTER 9: POLITICAL PROPAGANDA: TOOLS, MECHANISMS, AND WAYS TO AVOID IT.. 51
TECHNIQUES AND HOW POLITICAL PROPAGANDA WORKS 51
THE TOOLS OF PROPAGANDA 52
LOOKING INTO SOCIAL MEDIA TOOLS 52

CHAPTER 10: PSYCHOLOGICAL WARFARE: DON'T BE MANIPULATED 55
METHOD 1 – GAINING MANIPULATION SKILLS 55
METHOD 2 – USING DIFFERENT MANIPULATION TECHNIQUES 58

METHOD 3 – MANIPULATE ANYONE IN YOUR LIFE 61

HOW TO DEFEND YOURSELF FROM MANIPULATIVE INDIVIDUALS 65

CHAPTER 11: WORKSPACE MANIPULATORS: SPOT THEM AND STOP THEM 73

DECEPTION TACTICS AT THE WORKPLACE – HOW TO INFLUENCE PEOPLE 73

WHICH INFLUENCE TACTIC IS RIGHT FOR YOU? 74

GROW YOUR CORE LEADERSHIP SKILLS FOR EVERY ROLE 75

HACK OTHERS' MIND WITH COGNITIVE BIASES 78

WHAT IS THE BARNUM EFFECT? 79

HOW TO USE BARNUM STATEMENTS TO INFLUENCE PEOPLE 80

PART 3: UNLOCKING YOUR POWERS 81

CHAPTER 12: NLP: MASTER PERSUASION & NEGOTIATION TECHNIQUES 82

STATE CONTROL 82

WHAT ARE THE FUNDAMENTALS OF HUMAN BEHAVIOR AND CHANGE? 84

HOW TO SAFEGUARD YOURSELF FROM MANIPULATION/PERSUASION 86

CHAPTER 13: THE ANTIDOTE TO GROUPTHINK: 10 WAYS TO BEAT THE HERD 91

CHAPTER 14: BODY LANGUAGE: SPEED-READING AND SENDING OUT THE RIGHT MESSAGE 95

ANALYZING DIFFERENT BODY LANGUAGE 97

WATCH OUT FOR YOURSELF AND OTHERS 99

CHAPTER 15: CREATING YOUR OWN THOUGHTS 101

BENEFITS OF CREATING YOUR OWN THOUGHTS 103

TIPS TO IDENTIFY THAT YOU MAY NOT BE CREATING YOUR OWN THOUGHTS 104

CONCLUSION 105

SOURCES 106

SECTION 2: NLP 109

INTRODUCTION 110

PART 1: NLP ESSENTIALS 113

CHAPTER ONE: WHAT IS NEURO-LINGUISTIC PROGRAMMING? .113

- How NLP Was Founded 114
- The Early Development of NLP 114
- How NLP was Commercialized 116
- NLP- Its Underlying Principles 117
- NLP - Theoretical Model System 118
- Techniques of NLP 118
- The Test-Operate-Test-Exit Model (T.O.T.E. Model) of NLP 120
- Benefits of NLP 121

CHAPTER TWO: REFRAMING TO CHANGE YOUR MIND 124
- Reframing in NLP 124
- Types of Reframing – Content and Context 126
- Six Steps You Can Use to Master the Process of Reframing 127
- When Do You Use Reframing? 129
- Is Reframing A Form of Denial? 129
- Useful Tips for Reframing 130

CHAPTER THREE: ANCHORING TECHNIQUES TO CHANGE YOUR LIFE 131
- What is Anchoring? 131
- How Did Anchoring Originate? 132
- Common Anchors in Your Daily Life 133
- Types of Anchors 134
- The Process of Anchoring 134
- The Five Keys You Should Know About Successful Anchoring 136
- Applications of NLP Anchoring 137
- Is Anchoring Always Successful and Beneficial? 138

CHAPTER FOUR: CREATING RAPPORT 139
- What is Rapport? 139
- Why Is It Important to Focus on Building Rapport? 140
- Who Is It Applicable To? 141
- Three Steps to Build Rapport 142

BEHAVIORS AND ACTIONS TO MATCH AND MIRROR 143

PART 2: NLP PRACTICUM 147

CHAPTER FIVE: NLP TECHNIQUES TO PERSUADE ANYONE 147

WHAT IS PERSUASION? 148
NLP TECHNIQUES FOR PERSUASION 149
ADVANTAGES OF NLP 151
ESSENTIALS FOR PERSUASION 151

CHAPTER SIX: THE NLP NEGOTIATOR: EFFECTIVE TACTICS 153

SIX GOLDEN RULES FOR EFFECTIVE NEGOTIATOR 153
TOOLS FOR PERSUASION 157

CHAPTER SEVEN: CHAPTER SEVEN - BECOME A SOCIAL INFLUENCER THROUGH NLP 159

WHAT IS SOCIAL INFLUENCE? 159
USING NLP TO BECOME A SUCCESSFUL SOCIAL INFLUENCER 161
CAPTURING THE MIND OF THE AUDIENCE 164

CHAPTER EIGHT: TRANSFORMATIVE NLP FOR POSITIVITY AND CONFIDENCE 167

NLP FOR POSITIVITY AND CONFIDENCE 167
POWERFUL TOOL TO GET RID OF ANXIETY 171

CHAPTER NINE: SUCCESS NLP: GET WHAT YOU WANT NOW 173

THE COMPONENTS OF NLP 174
THE THREE STEPS TO SUCCESS 176
WHAT IS THE DRIVING FORCE IN LIFE? 178
THE BIGGEST ENEMY 179
THE LAW OF IDENTITY AND FACTORS THAT INFLUENCE YOUR IDENTITY 179

PART 3: DARK NLP 182

CHAPTER TEN: IS NLP A FORM OF MANIPULATION? 182

WHAT IS MANIPULATION? 182
HOW TO USE NLP AS A USEFUL TOOL TO MANIPULATE 183

CHAPTER ELEVEN: THE KIND MANIPULATOR 186

MANIPULATION TECHNIQUES THAT AREN'T SO BAD! 186

CHAPTER TWELVE: NLP TECHNIQUES IN MASS MIND CONTROL (MEDIA, POLITICS & CULTS) 192
- Governments and Media 193
- Advertising and Marketing 195
- Social Media 198
- Cults 199

CHAPTER THIRTEEN: SEDUCTIVE NLP LANGUAGE 201
- Techniques in Seduction 202

CHAPTER FOURTEEN: AVOIDING NLP MIND CONTROL (AND THINKING FOR YOURSELF) 208
- Seven Ways to Manipulate 208
- How to Defend Yourself from NLP Mind Control 210
- Who Uses It? 210
- How Do You Make Sure that You Aren't Being Manipulated? 211
- How to Think for Yourself 212
- Ways to Think on Your Own 213
- Advantages of Thinking on Your Own 214

CONCLUSION 215

REFERENCES 217

Section 1: Dark Psychology

Master Persuasion, Negotiation, and NLP and Unlock the Power of Understanding Manipulation, Deception, and Human Behavior

Introduction

The world is full of chaos because of the Dark Triad traits. In this book, we will discuss each of the "Dark Triad" personality traits, and they include psychopathy, Machiavellianism, and narcissism. People with some of these traits are fond of manipulating other people that may seem vulnerable to some extent. When a person manipulates another individual, they are focusing on fulfilling their selfish interests. If you are a vulnerable individual, you should focus on learning more about the "Dark Triad" traits.

In this book, you will also learn more about some of the deception tactics used by these individuals. By reading through this dark psychology handbook, you will learn more about the human mind and behavior. Also, you will get to learn more about how people have mastered the art of manipulating their colleagues for their benefit.

By reading through this book, you will also learn more about how you can analyze a person's character and how you can differentiate between the truth and a lie. You will also learn more about how different traits affect the human race. At times, people try to understand others. It may be quite challenging; however, this book will ensure that you have learned more about different issues affecting humanity, including cults and mind control. This handbook will also look at the role of manipulation within the workplace and the family setting. The phenomena refers to how people deceive others, coercing them into doing their bidding. After reading through this book, you will learn more about the traits possessed by malicious individuals. Also, you will learn more about the traits of a person affected by psychopathy, Machiavellianism, and narcissism.

This book will act as your first step to understanding what is required of you when you want to evade people who use manipulation techniques, to stop them from ruining your life. Since the world is turning into a chaotic place, the information in this book will ensure that you can handle different critical issues that may be affecting you as an individual. You can also understand the instances of being abused by close people in your life.

Also, you will learn more about how to defend and safeguard yourself from deception and manipulation. Finally, you will understand more about how to handle vulnerable people effectively in case they need your assistance as a professional. Although many books talk about Dark Psychology, we are happy that you have chosen this specific handbook. I hope that the book is informative, although we have not discussed the entire field of Dark Psychology. We will dig further into the field of Dark Psychology with time. Enjoy your read!

PART 1: The Dark Side

Chapter 1: Dark Psychology: The Dark Triad

People have different personality traits. It is hard to deal with people who are arrogant, volatile, and also domineering. When dealing with certain characters, you should be careful, and you can work on neutralizing their behavior, while also ensuring that you have restored harmony.

There are some characteristics and behaviors that may be seriously damaging, and when a person displays these toxic traits, they may end up undermining their colleagues. Also, some of these traits may end up poisoning and destroying a team. The "Dark Triad" of personality traits comprises of psychopathy, narcissism, and Machiavellianism. In this chapter, the focus will be on these three elements. We will identify all the behaviors associated with each of these elements. Also, we will look at the impact of each of these elements in the workplace.

About the Dark Triad

The "Dark Triad" is not a commonly used phrase in the field of psychology. The term refers to three personality traits, and they may be related to some extent. The personality traits include narcissism, Machiavellianism, and psychopathy.

Narcissism – the term is derived from the Greek myth about the character known as Narcissus; he was a hunter, and he ended up falling in love with his own reflection, while observing himself in a pool of water. He ended up drowning as a result. According to the myth, narcissistic people are normally selfish, arrogant, boastful, and hypersensitive, especially when they are criticized.

Psychopathy – there are different personality traits associated with psychopathy, and they include lack of remorse, lack of empathy, being volatile and manipulative, and antisocial behavior. There is a huge difference between being a psychopath and having psychopathic traits. Psychopathy is normally related to criminal violence.

Machiavellianism – the word is derived from an Italian politician known as Niccolo Machiavelli. He gained a lot of recognition as the author of a book known as *The Prince,* published in 1532. People who have read the book can ascertain that it endorses the dark arts that are associated with deceit and cunning behavior. The traits associated with Machiavellianism include manipulation, duplicity, a lack of morality and emotion, and self-interest.

How to Identify Dark Triad Traits

To identify the Dark Triad traits, psychologists need to measure different personality types. In 2010, Dr. Peter Jonason developed and published a rating scale known as *The Dirty Dozen: A Concise Measure of the Dark Triad* with Gregory Webster, a professional psychologist. The rating scale comprises of a 12-item methodology, and it comes in handy when measuring the dark traits. Psychologists normally ask people to rate themselves using the following questions:

- I tend to lack remorse.
- I have used flattery to get my way.
- I tend to want others to pay attention to me.
- I tend to want others to admire me.
- I tend to exploit others toward my own ends.
- I tend to seek prestige or status.

- I tend to expect special favors from others.
- I tend to be cynical.
- I have used deceit or lied to get my way.
- I tend to manipulate others to get my way.
- I tend not to be too concerned with morality or the morality of my actions.
- I tend to be callous or insensitive.

At a basic level, a person can be rated from one to seven, although the rating scale has twelve questions. The possible score is from 12 to 84. A higher score indicates that a person may possess some of the Dark Triad traits.

Managing People with Dark Triad Traits

If you usually exhibit the Dark Triad traits, you may be wondering whether there is something that you can do about it. The answer to how the Dark Triad traits can be managed is quite complex. Experienced psychologists can weigh into the matter. For starters, when looking into different personality types, you will notice that there are many gradations. A person's behavior can change daily. As a manager, you will have to look into ways that you can address some of the associated negative behaviors so that you can ensure that your team works in harmony, and their productivity levels will also be good.

How to Cope with Anger

There may be some team members who have some psychopathic traits, and they may be prone to aggression and anger. Such situations should be handled quickly. First, make sure that you are conversant with the signs of anger. Normal anger can be spotted easily. For instance, when a person is angry, they may raise their voice, and they may also begin to sweat in the process. Some people try to suppress their anger, and they will showcase some "passive-aggressiveness," and it entails ignoring people, among other things.

Some strategies come in handy when dealing with angry people. If you feel threatened, you should first ensure that you are safe. For instance, you can leave the room instantly. When dealing with a person who has anger issues, you should ensure that you have distanced yourself from these individuals emotionally. Also, make sure that you have identified the cause of the anger. You can become an active listener and also use questioning techniques.

How to Deal with Bullying

At times, anger may roll over to bullying. Bullying is associated with threatening behavior and verbal abuse. It can include unnecessary criticism, spreading some malicious rumors, and belittling someone. It can also be behavior that treats a person as if they are "invisible." If you notice that there is a bully within a specific team, you should start by according the victim some support. Also, you should go ahead and confront the bully while holding them accountable for the damage they have caused.

Spotting a Manipulator

People in the workplace can be influenced in different ways. For instance, you can encourage a person and also praise them depending on the good work that they have done. By inspiring people in the workplace, you will increase the employees' productivity. If one of the team members has some Machiavellian tendencies, they will try to bring about some undue influence on the employees at the workplace by trying to manipulate them. They may also try to coerce the employees through deception.

A manipulative person will always try to hide their behavior, and there are some signs that you should always look out for, such as dealing with a person who cannot take "no" for an answer. Manipulative people will always depict some hurtful behavior when dealing with different people, since they always have some malicious motives.

When you try to challenge a manipulative person, you should be specific about some of the actions that you have spotted. Also, look into how the manipulative person is harming your team. You should go ahead and make it clear to such a person that their behavior cannot be tolerated and that they should change for the better. It is advisable to sign a performance agreement. Such as agreement will ensure that the manipulative person is held accountable in case their actions jeopardize the production levels of the team members.

Dealing with Narcissism

Narcissists are usually selfish, and they can be more of a headache to deal with. They do not pose a major threat; however, when they disrupt the team's morale and harmony, they may fail to realize that they have some undue influence on the team members. It is good to raise such an issue as early as possible after you have realized that there is something wrong.

Narcissists have different character traits, including having a big ego. They can also do anything to gain recognition. They can also demand credit for different ideas that they may have come up with. Despite working with other people as a team, they will go ahead and take credit for the idea as an individual. They also try to dominate meetings and discussions.

A person with a huge ego will not expect to be challenged by another person. When challenging a narcissist, you should make sure that you have stood your ground. You should also arm yourself with some solid counter-arguments. It is also advisable to put a narcissist in a situation whereby they are dependent on the cooperation from other colleagues. By doing so, you will increase the level of understanding and respect among your peers.

Building the Skills that You May Need to Cope

It is not easy to imagine and accept that there exist people with negative behaviors. Also, you may experience some challenges when you are not very confident about winning an argument against another person. There are numerous ways through which you can build on the skills that you need to cope with some of these challenges. For instance, you can learn how to be assertive.

If you have some of these "Dark Triad" personality traits, there are many things that you can do so that you can gain the ability to understand people in a better manner. Also, you can learn more about recognizing a person's emotional perspective and state. You can try to boost your "people skills" by building emotional intelligence and empathy. You should also be aware of people's body language. Additionally, you can manage your emotions using some of these skills. You will also have a greater understanding of how people can help you as you try to spot your patterns comprising of unwanted behavior before you turn into a threat to other team members.

The Impact of the Dark Triad at the Workplace

It is hard to find anything positive relating to the Dark Triad traits, especially at the workplace. People with Dark Triad traits will always display undesirable behavior such as being volatile, aggressive, deceitful, and selfish. Some people may also display a combination of these traits. Various psychologists have been looking into the impact of the Dark Triad. Dr. Seth Spain composed a paper in 2014 named, *The Dark Side of Personality at Work*. In the paper, he stated that there is a relationship between unethical decision-making practices in the workplace and Machiavellianism. Other researchers who have weighed into the matter include Kevin M. Williams and Delroy L. Paulhus, in their 2002 study *The Dark Triad of personality:*

Narcissism, Machiavellianism, and psychopathy. Both psychologists argue that some tendencies are associated with Machiavellianism, narcissism, and psychopathy; nevertheless, each of these traits are independent entities. Further research has also been carried out, and there is a huge correlation between lack of humility and dishonesty.

Peter Jonason's 2012 study *The Dark Triad at work: how toxic employees get their way* – with co-authors Sarah Slomski and Jamie Partyka, showcases that employees with Dark Triad traits are usually "toxic" individuals. For instance, the "toxic" employees may bring about some undue influence over other people at the workplace. With time, some of the employees may showcase some aggressiveness, and they may also try to influence people forcefully.

There is evidence that narcissism can be viewed, especially initially, from a positive perspective. In most cases, narcissists make an effort with their appearance and usually are friendly and charming. They will also be achievement-oriented and conscientious, and all these things usually reflect well on an individual. With time, their self-absorbed "me, me, me" attitude may become tiresome.

Guarding Yourself Against the Undue Influence of Dark Triad Individuals

Some psychologists have managed to compose books on how people can safeguard themselves from the undue influence brought about by individuals with Dark Triad traits. According to psychologists such as Oliver James, in his 2013 book *Office Politics: How to Thrive in a World of Lying, Backstabbing and Dirty Tricks,* the Dark Triad tendencies ensure that some employees in the workplace have a nefarious advantage concerning their progression and career growth. When a person is "triadic," they usually exhibit all the traits associated with the Dark Triad, which can help to advance their careers through bullying and manipulating their way up the organization. Some business professionals use the term "think greedy," and the main focus is on attaining their goals regardless of the cost.

Patrick Fagan is an associate lecturer at the University of London, and he has an in-depth understanding of consumer behaviors. According to Patrick Fagan, the Dark Triad traits can help a person to work their way up an organization even if they are unable to get along with other employees. A narcissist will always have high self-esteem, and they may be yearning for the leadership positions within an organization. Psychopathic people will also focus more on being high-achievers, and they will not be concerned about whether their ambitions affect the people around them. As for the Machiavellians, they tend to portray themselves as good people but are manipulative.

The Dark Triad traits can also bring about "corporate psychopaths," who have a diminished sense of collective responsibility. According to Clive Boddy, a University professor with a doctorate in corporate psychopathy, some of these personality types are common in the finance sector and the civil service.

A person with the Dark Triad traits will always put their needs before those of any other individual within the workplace. The tendencies of people with Dark Triad traits may bring down the organization. If one of the leaders within the organization has showcased Dark Triad traits, the organization cannot easily prosper. If you are a manager, you should always be on the lookout for people with Dark Triad traits. You should deal with such individuals vigorously and guard the other employees against their influence. At times, you may have to remove people from the organization when they exhibit some unwanted characteristics.

Key Points

We had earlier discussed the Dark Triad personality traits, and they include Machiavellianism, Narcissism, and psychopathy. All of these traits are associated with toxicity, and a person with such traits can easily wreak havoc at the workplace. You should always be aware that a person possessing such traits might be a high-achiever, and they may also potentially be charming and achievement-oriented.

Some tools may come in handy when identifying a Dark Triad personality. If you are not a skilled psychologist, you should not attempt to carry out such an assessment individually. If you have noticed some negative behavior from some team members, you should liaise with the human resource manager, and they will look into the matter. Your main responsibility is to ensure that you have managed the impact brought about by the negative behaviors of some employees at the workplace. You should not diagnose any individual in the workplace.

Negative and damaging behaviors should be addressed vigorously and actively. Some of the skills that you may need when dealing with a person with Dark Triad traits include emotional intelligence, assertiveness, and conflict management.

Chapter 2: The Nine Dark Personality Traits

You may know people who are narcissists; however, other character traits may be somewhat intriguing and less well known. According to the study *Measuring the Dark Core of Personality,* by Morten Moshagen, Ingo Zettler, and Benjamin E. Hilbig, (2020), there are nine dark personality traits, and they may be related since they come from a common root. If a person has one of these traits, it is an indicator that they may possess more of the dark personality traits. The study that talked about the nine dark personality traits was published in a peer-reviewed journal. The traits include:

- **Egoism** – this is the preoccupation associated with a person's achievement at the expense of other people.
- **Machiavellianism** – this trait is associated with being manipulative, having a bad attitude, and believing that the end justifies the means.
- **Moral disagreement** – this is the ability to behave in an unethical manner without feeling bad about the outcome.
- **Narcissism** – this trait is associated with superiority, excessive self-absorption, and the extreme need for attention.

- **Psychological entitlement** – this is the belief that you are superior to your counterparts.
- **Psychopathy** – this trait is associated with impulsivity and a lack of empathy.
- **Sadism** – this is the desire to inflict physical or mental harm on other people and also deriving some pleasure from this.
- **Self-interest** – this is the desire to boost your own financial and social status.
- **Spitefulness** – this is a trait associated with the willingness to harm others, and you may also derive some joy from harming yourself.

While studying different individuals, psychologists have been able to identify people with different Dark Triad traits. There was an overlap, and the people who scored a higher rating in one area had a high likelihood of having a higher rating in other areas.

According to the study's authors Moshagen, Zettler, and Hilbig, the root of all these traits is known as the "D-factor," and it can be defined as the "tendency to maximize your utility regardless of the repercussions." The root motivation of people with Dark Triad traits is that they will always put themselves before other people.

For instance, the D-factor is evident in cases of rule-breaking, extreme violence, deception within a company, and lying. If you have learned more about how to assess a person's D-factor, you can easily look into whether a person can engage in different malicious acts.

Different psychologists have written about the D-factor, and it is somewhat similar to the "g" factor of intelligence. According to the g-factor, when a person has a high score in a certain area of intelligence, there is a high likelihood that they will also have a high score in other areas.

In the same way, a high score in one area of the Dark Triad normally goes hand in hand with a high score in other areas. Some of the attempts to explain the Dark Triad traits see them as "indicators" of an adaptive evolutionary strategy that is directed toward gratification and gaining immediate awards. Also, these traits can be associated with reproductive benefits and the survival of a person.

As for the "D-factor," it is quite complicated, and it is more encompassing since it may have other explanations.

What remains to be seen in this case? More research has to be carried out so that we may learn more about the Dark Triad Traits and how they are related, including research focusing more on how each of these traits develop gradually in a person's life. The findings are somewhat intuitive, and studies normally go a long way in showing that all these traits are interconnected, even if we have not gained a full understanding of the interconnection in this case.

Chapter 3: Dark Criminals Among Us

Before a person orchestrates something malicious, they may have thought about everything for a prolonged period, for instance, in the case of a mass shooting. The perpetrator's main motive may be unknown; however, it is evident upon investigation that such people have usually engaged in negative behaviors that are harmful to others close to them.

Some researchers, such as James Alan Fox and Monica J. DeLateur in their paper *Mass Shootings in America: Moving Beyond Newtown* (2013), have looked into the matter, and the difficulty of identifying a potential mass shooter in advance, especially at a tender age. Nevertheless, it is evident that there are some thinking patterns and behaviors that usually manifest with time, and educators also encounter them since they spend a considerable amount of time with pupils. The parents are also familiar with each of these patterns. The main hope is that the children who exhibit each of these traits can outgrow them eventually. Some children do; however, some do not outgrow these traits, and they can harm the people around them. When the patterns intensify, it is important to seek help, and we cannot wait for a seriously malicious action to occur.

When a person engages in crime at a tender age, it is a sign that there is some trouble ahead; not necessarily a mass shooting, however, the behaviors of such people may result in other people being financially, emotionally, and physically hurt.

People with Dark Triad traits may also engage in lying while also blaming other people for their misfortunes. The parents and teachers may not have the ability to control some of the choices that the children make; nevertheless, they may have noticed some warning signs.

Although Dark Triad traits manifest over time, children who simply exhibit some of these traits cannot be labeled as "criminals," since they have not done anything wrong. Since the children are still young, they may still be learning about the world and they can develop more understanding and empathy as they grow. They can turn out as good, well-rounded people, so it is important to support and work with them, without labelling children negatively.

Children are delicate beings, and they should be molded accordingly. When a child is born, people strive to look into whether the child may have learning problems, physical disabilities, and emotional problems. We should also strive to ensure that we have identified other problems that the children may be suffering from so that they cannot injure their peers or cause any harm to themselves, since they do not have any sense of responsibility at a young age, this comes with learning and maturity.

The mental health system should be improved. There should be some strict background checks, and gun laws should also be revised. We should also focus more on identifying some of the "errors" present in the thinking process. We all possess enough knowledge about how we can help children who show potentially harmful traits. The children can be mentored accordingly, and they can hopefully develop more positive traits in the future. Always embark on such a mission with sensitivity and compassion.

Criminal Mind vs. Cybercriminal Mind

In this section, we will look into the cybercriminal mind and the criminal mind. Criminal psychology is also known as criminological psychology, and it is the study of the thoughts, views, actions, and intentions of people that engage in different forms of criminal behavior. The study is related to criminal anthropology, and it delves deep into what drives someone into becoming a criminal. Additionally, the study also looks into a person's reactions after committing a crime.

Criminal psychologists are frequently called up to the stand in court so that they may serve as witnesses, since they have an in-depth understanding of the criminal mind. There are different types of psychiatry, and they also deal with some aspects of criminal behavior. Criminal behavior can be termed as any form of antisocial behavior that is also punishable by the law and the norms within a community. It is, however, somewhat difficult to define the criminal mind.

The Role of Psychology in the Legal System

Psychologists and psychiatrists are normally professionals who are licensed, and they are tasked with assessing the physical and mental state of a person. There are also profilers, and they are tasked with looking for patterns in a person's behavior as they try to identify the person who took part in a certain crime. Some group efforts also focus more on attempting to answer different "common" psychological questions. If a sexual offender is about to commit a re-offending act after being put back into society, how can such an issue be handled? Other issues that arise include; is the sexual offender fit enough to take the stand in court? Was the offender sane when they were committing the offense?

A criminal psychologist may be required to undertake investigative tasks such as examining photographs that were taken at a crime scene. They can also be tasked with interviewing the victim and the suspect.

At times, a criminal psychologist comes up with a hypothesis to assess what the offender might do after being released after they have completed their sentence.

The question about a person's competency to stand trial depends on the offender's state of mind as they engaged in the criminal act, and when they are about to take the stand in court. The criminal psychologist will have to assess the ability of the offender to understand the charges that have been placed against them and the possible outcomes that may arise after they are convicted. The offender should also have the ability to offer some assistance to their attorneys as they defend them in court.

The question of criminal responsibility is aimed at assessing the criminal's state of mind as they committed the crime. The main focus is on whether they understand the difference between what is right and wrong and anything that is against the law. The insanity defense is not commonly used, since it cannot be proved easily. If a person succeeds with the insanity defense, they will be sent to a secure hospital facility for a long period as compared to the period that they would have served in prison.

The Roles of a Criminal Psychologist

The roles of a legal psychologist are as follows:

Clinical – In such an instance, the psychologist is supposed to assess an individual so that they can issue a clinical judgment. The psychologist can make use of different assessment tools, psychometric tools, or they can take part in a normal interview with the offender. After that, they are supposed to make an informed decision depending on the outcome of the interview. The assessment comes in handy since it can help the police and other organizations to determine how the offender, in this case, will be processed. For instance, the clinical psychologist can find out whether the offender is sane so that they can stand a trial. They can also determine whether the offender has a mental illness, which relates to whether they are capable of understanding the court proceedings.

Experimental – In this instance, the psychologist is tasked with carrying out some research about the case. They can perform some experiments so that they can illustrate a certain point while also providing further information that will be presented as evidence in court. They may carry out eye-witness credibility and false memory assessments. For instance, they can try to assess whether an eye-witness can spot an object that is 100 meters away.

Advisory – A psychologist is supposed to advise the police about how they should proceed with the investigation. For instance, they can weigh into matters such as which is the best way to interview an eye-witness and the offender. They can also weigh into matters such as how an offender may act after committing a crime.

Actuarial – This is where the psychologist makes use of statistics so that they can inform a case. For instance, they can be tasked with providing the probability of an event taking place. The court may also consider the likelihood of a person engaging in certain acts such as defiling another person sexually after they have served their jail term or after they have been released, if the evidence against them was not strong enough.

Profiling

Criminal profiling is also referred to as offender profiling. It is the process of linking the actions of an offender to the crime scene. The offender's characteristics will also ensure that the police can prioritize and narrow down all possibilities when considering all of the possible suspects. Profiling is quite new concerning forensic psychology. The field of forensic psychology has grown in the past two decades. Initially, it was an art. Currently, it is a rigorous science. There are different sub-fields in forensic psychology, including investigative psychology. Criminal profiling currently entails carrying out some intensive research and also carrying out some rigorous methodological advances.

Criminals are usually classified based on factors such as sex, age, physical characteristics, geographic region, and education. When comparing some of the similar characteristics, you can easily understand a criminal's motivation when they decide to partake in criminal behavior.

Some national and international security organizations, including the FBI, usually refer to "criminal profiling" as "criminal investigative analysis." The analysts or profilers are normally trained. During the training process, they learn more about the behavioral aspects of different people, and also learn more about the details of unsolved violent crime scenes, whereby there are some traces of psychopathy at the scene where the crime was committed.

A good profiler should be able to deduce the following characteristics after arriving at the crime scene:
1. The amount of planning that went into the crime.
2. The degree of control depicted by the offender.
3. The escalation of emotion at the crime scene.
4. The risk level of the victim and the offender.
5. The general appearance of the crime scene. It may be organized or disorganized.

The profiler can go ahead and interpret the behavior of the offender based on the crime scene. They can discuss everything further with their counterparts.

As a criminal psychologist, you may have to consider profiling from a racial perspective. Race plays a major role in the criminal justice system. In the past few years, the state and federal prisons have held more than 475,900 black inmates. The number of white inmates totaled 436,500. The difference is quite significant. Some of the black people are in prison because of negative stereotypes. Such stereotypes are ineffective, and some criminal psychologists can ascertain that the race of a person does not contribute to them being violent.

There are environmental, cultural, and traditional concepts that surround each race. Each of these concepts plays a key role in psychology. Some people may lack equal opportunities as a result of race or gender, for example, and that means that they have less chances to thrive. Psychologists also try to evaluate whether prison is the most stable place for certain criminals since they may have committed certain offenses as a result of mental illnesses that were not addressed earlier.

Applied Criminal Psychology

For a criminal psychiatrist, the main question is, "Which offender will become a patient?" and "Which patient will become an offender?" Other questions that a psychiatrist should ask themselves is, "Which came first, the mental disorder or the crime?" Psychologists should take a look into the environmental factors and the genetics of a person while they carry out the profiling, to help determine whether the suspect committed the crime or not.

Some of the questions that criminal psychologists should ask themselves include:

- Is the mental disorder present at the moment? Did the person have the mental disorder when they were engaging in the criminal act?
- What is the level of responsibility of the person who committed the crime?
- Is treatment the best option when trying to reduce the risks of reoffending?
- Is there a possibility that the offender may engage in another crime, and what are the risk factors in this case?

The individual psychiatric evaluations normally come in handy since they help to measure an offender's personality traits through psychological testing. The results can also be presented in court.

Chapter 4: Quiz: Are You a Dark Personality?

Some tests have been formulated over the years, and they come in handy when measuring the "Dark Triad" traits.

Introduction

The "Dark Triad" personality traits are three in total. Although each of these traits is independent, they are all closely related, and they may have some malevolent connection. The three traits include Machiavellianism (having a manipulative attitude), psychopathy (lack of empathy), and narcissism (excessive self-love). The Dark Triad is normally assessed depending on each of these mentioned traits. The "Dark Triad" traits can also be tested individually. To measure narcissism, psychologists would make use of the NPI (Narcissistic Personality Inventory). The MACH-IV was used to measure Machiavellianism, and psychopathy was measured using the LSRP (Levenson Self-Report Psychopathy Scale). The differences between each of these tests are present in their analysis aspect. One test that was developed recently includes the *Short Dark Triad (SD3): A Brief Measure of Dark Personality Traits,* developed by Daniel N. Jones and Delroy L. Paulhus in 2013, and it comes in handy since it produces a uniform assessment.

Procedure

This is a test that is comprised of 26 statements that should be rated depending on how much a person agrees with them. The test should not take a lot of time. It is possible to complete the test in about five minutes.

Participation

This assessment should only be used for educational purposes. The results of the test should not be used when offering psychological advice. If you are interested in learning more about the "Dark Triad" personality traits, and how each trait should be assessed, you should not take this participation test, you should seek advice from a trained professional. This informal test is used for research purposes and should be taken anonymously.

	Disagree	Neutral	Agree
People see me as a natural leader.			
It's not wise to tell your secrets.			
Payback needs to be quick and nasty.			
I avoid dangerous situations.			
I like to use clever manipulation to get my way.			
Many group activities tend to be dull without me.			
It's wise to keep track of information that you can			

use against people later.			
I insist on getting the respect I deserve.			
I hate being the center of attention.			
There are things you should hide from other people because they don't need to know.			
I like to get revenge on authorities.			
People often say I'm out of control.			
I am an average person.			
Whatever it takes, you must get the important people on your side.			
You should wait for the right time to get back to people.			
I'll say anything to get what I want.			
Make sure your plans benefit you, not others.			
I have never gotten into trouble with the law.			
I know that I am special because everyone keeps telling me so.			

Most people can be manipulated.			
Avoid direct conflict with others because they may be useful in the future.			
People who mess with me always regret it.			
I like to get acquainted with important people.			
I enjoy having sex with people I hardly know.			
I have been compared to famous people.			
It's true that I can be mean to others.			

As per the table above, your answer is graded from 1-3. The results are always issued after you have answered all of the questions in the quiz.

PART 2: Mind Control, Deception, and Manipulation

Chapter 5: Creepy Facts about Mind Control

Mind Control – the term refers to the controversial theory that proposes that it is possible to influence a person's thinking, emotions, behavior, and decisions by outside sources. Mind control is also referred to as "reeducation," "brainwashing," and "coercive persuasion," as well as "brain sweeping," "thought reform" and "thought control."

Creepy Facts about Mind Control

Cults – there are different cults throughout the globe, and they usually focus on brainwashing their followers through mind control. Some well-known cults are self-proclaimed churches and other religious movements. Each cult makes use of different mind control techniques, including isolation and sleep deprivation, in a bid to weaken the mental state of the target, and also to make people susceptible to different religious indoctrinations.

In some cases, the people who have been indoctrinated into one of these churches are first subjected to biblical teachings continuously for about 21 days. The teaching sessions are normally intense, and they usually override a person's ability to view reality as it is, and the cult leaders then take advantage of their followers. The cult leaders succeed in their endeavors by fully overriding a person's thoughts, critical thinking skills, emotions, thoughts, and behavior.

Toxoplasma/Toxoplasmosis – this is a single-celled organism, and there is growing evidence that it can alter a person's behavior. The parasite normally affects living things such as rats, and it can alter their behavior so that they are less risk averse; for example, they can be less afraid of predators like cats. The parasite can also affect humans. When humans consume contaminated meat, soil, or cat poo, they can come become infected with the parasite.

The Devil's Breath – the term was derived from a tree in Colombia known as the Borrachero tree. Scopolamine is thought to affect people who come into contact with it, and they enter into a zombie state when the dust is blown into their faces. The symptoms of the devil's breath include loss of free will, confusion, and memory loss.

When a person is exposed to the devil's breath, they normally become susceptible. Some people claim they have committed crimes while they are under the influence of the devil's breath. When a person engages in a crime under the influence of this drug, they may fail to remember exactly what happened. For instance, an attacker may drug you, and you may end up heeding all their demands. Some attackers may lure you in such a way that you will take them to your home, and they will go ahead and take all the valuables present in the house.

Psychosurgery – this is a controversial means used to treat different psychological disorders. The procedure was administered using a blunt rod through the eye or the temple, and part of the brain tissue would be destroyed. The procedure was commonly referred to as lobotomy, and it was used to treat people who had mental disorders such as schizophrenia. After undergoing the psychosurgery, the patients would become calmer; however, they would exhibit some severe side effects, including memory loss, loss of emotions, child-like behavior, and reduced intellectual functioning. Psychosurgery is still used in the modern era; however, it is used as a last resort.

The Remote-Control Bull – the technique was invented by Dr. Jose Delgado in 1963, and he was able to control bulls using a chip that would be implanted into the brain of the bull. When the bull started to charge, Delgado would use a remote button to stop the bull. The chip would use a "stimoceiver," and it would stimulate some parts of the brain. Some researchers have been looking into the experiments carried out by Dr. Delgado, and they are bound to improve the technology greatly. With time, they can use the technique on animals such as rats, sharks, and pigeons.

Mind-Controlled Delusions – some researchers have been using hypnosis while investigating delusions and psychosis in healthy people. Using hypnosis, a scientist can take control of a person's mind to cause them to hallucinate, while recording the effect of the hypnosis on each patient. While hypnotized, the patients normally have an out of body experience, and they normally feel that they are being manipulated like puppets by a puppeteer.

Hypno-mugging – there are some instances where people have been mugged after being hypnotized. For instance, a thief may act friendly, and after a few minutes, they can put you in a trance. When a robber learns more about hypnosis, they can easily attack different people, and they can frisk them in broad daylight. Hypnosis is not a common technique when it comes to mugging people.

MK-ULTRA – this is the name of a code that refers to different experiments that were carried out by the CIA during the 1950s. The experiments were carried out using different methods such as psychoactive drugs, sensory deprivation, and isolation, and the main focus was on altering a person's brain functions and mental state – the program aimed at creating spies against their own will. The MK-ULTRA program managed to manipulate the mental state of different people.

Subliminal Messages – "subliminal messaging" refers to the ability to pass a message to another person, and they will not be able to recognize the message consciously. There have been some reports that there are some subliminal messages in films and advertisements.

Some music videos also contain subliminal messages. The messages, in this case, may relate to purchasing different products, for example. But these kinds of subconscious messages could potentially have a more sinister effect, depending on the message. Over the years, there have been many debates about subliminal messages.

Ultrasound Soldiers – the United States government has a research agency known as DARPA. The agency is normally funded by the government so that it may develop army helmets that can be used to inflict mind control using ultrasound frequencies.

Mind control is possible depending on the areas of the brain that are being stimulated. It is hoped that the click of a button can manipulate the mind of a soldier as a way of enhancing their fighting capabilities as they go to war. The ultrasonic devices are supposed to be embedded in the helmets that are to be worn by the soldiers, and they can, in turn, transform the soldiers into an unstoppable fighting machine. In theory, the brains of soldiers can be stimulated, and they will not feel any pain, fatigue, or fear. Researchers have been looking into the matter, and they are currently conducting some experiments using worms. At the moment, it is possible to control the direction that the worms travel by using the ultrasound technology that might eventually be used to control soldiers on the battlefield.

Many myths have come up over the years about brainwashing and mind control. As a student, you may be used to analyzing various problems from a certain angle, and you can make your own conclusions in the process.

Daily Mind Control

As a marketer, your focus may be on how you can manipulate different people using different techniques, so that they may bend to your will. Some of the daily mind control techniques that people are subjected to include:

The color of a pill may trick you into thinking that it works effectively.

The scenario in the film *The Matrix* (1999), saw the character Neo being asked to choose between the "red" and "blue" pill. The blue pill would put him to sleep, yet the red pill would ensure that he woke up to "reality." This could be a comment on the apparent psychological impact of color, as many sleeping pills at the pharmacy are indeed blue.

Some people may assume that it is the placebo effect. In this case, the way you perceive different things matters a lot, especially regarding the products that we consume.

MK-ULTRA

The Korean War took place in the 1950s. The war wasn't easy for the United States, and the nation was experiencing some serious challenges, especially when dealing with the Soviet Union. The United States had to look for a way to win the war, and that is when it focused on the human brain. In 1952, the CIA was being led by Allen Dulles. As the director of the CIA, he went ahead to express his concerns about the war.

About MK-Ultra

As the CIA Director, Dulles went ahead to come up with the MK-Ultra Program. The program was classified, and it entailed the use of chemical and biological weapons, sensory deprivation, hypnosis, verbal and sexual abuse, and isolation. Whenever the United States captured a prisoner of war, they would torture them to gain information about the enemy. The prisoners of war would then be rendered incapacitated.

The MK-Ultra program aimed at coming up with a "truth serum" to force information from people who were suspected of being Soviet spies. The CIA was hopeful that it would increase a person's ability to recall some complex pieces of information and the arrangement of various physical objects. The main goals of the MK-Ultra program were to:

1. Produce shock and confusion over extended periods.

2. Cause a victim to age faster or slower.

3. Make it impossible for someone to perform physical activity.

4. Enhance the ability to withstand privation, torture, and coercion during interrogation.

5. Promote illogical thinking and impulsiveness so that a recipient would be discredited in public.

6. Lower ambition and working efficiency.

7. Weaken or distort eyesight or hearing.

8. Increase mental activity and perception.

9. Knock someone out with the use of surreptitiously administered drugs in drinks, food, cigarettes, or as an aerosol.

10. Alter personality structure causing the recipient to become dependent upon another person.

11. Cause temporary or permanent brain damage and loss of memory.

12. Produce physical disablement, such as paralysis of the legs.

13. Produce amnesia for events both preceding and during the experiments and the use of a prisoner.

About LSD

The CIA was conducting MK-Ultra research in colleges, universities, and pharmaceutical companies in North America. The CIA has expressed a specific interest in LSD (lysergic acid diethylamide). The medicine was first discovered in Switzerland, and the drug induces a mental state that is similar to depersonalization, schizophrenia, disintegration, and psychic disorganization. The main effect of the drug was that it could breakdown a person's character defenses for handling instances of anxiety.

The CIA would then administer the drug to its own employees, doctors, military personnel, and government agents without prior knowledge. By doing so, the CIA had violated the Nuremberg Code. The code was introduced after World War II, and it was meant to ensure that human trials would cease. At some point, prisoners were also part of the human trials. People who took LSD would experience a loss of appetite, paranoia, and they would also hallucinate.

Chapter 6: Deception Detection: How to Identify a Lie

Detecting Deception

There are different ways through which you can detect deception in an oral or written statement.

How to Detect an Anomaly

Some professionals have an in-depth understanding of linguistic text analysis. The analysis will entail studying the grammar, language, and syntax, and the main agenda is to learn more about how an event is described, in a bid to detect any anomalies. As an experienced investigator, you will be tasked with detecting some of the nonverbal cues of the subjects. You will focus on eye movement and verbal behavior. Oral statements will also be studied.

Signs of Deception

Some of the signs of deception are as follows:

1. The Lack of Self-Reference

If a person is truthful, they will utilize the pronoun "I" when they are describing what took place. For example, an honest person will go ahead and say, "I arrived home and went straight to the bedroom. After that, I went to talk to my mother, and we had a lengthy chat." That's just an example statement. As we can see, the pronoun "I" appears twice in the statement provided.

Deceptive people will use language that minimizes the number of "I" references. During an oral statement, the witness or suspect may end up leaving out some important pieces of information; this can happen even when they are issuing an informal written statement.

2. Answering a Question with a Question

Even though a person may be a liar, they will prefer not to engage in the act of lying. When a person lies, they risk being detected. Before you answer a question with a lie, you should avoid answering the question at all costs. When trying to act dodgy, people may often answer a question with another question. The investigators should always be on the lookout for people that answer a question with another question.

After talking about deception, we will now look into how to spot a liar. Since the FBI is a security organization, it is well suited to weighing into the matter on how to spot a liar. The following tips may come in handy when spotting a liar:

1. Focus on Building Rapport

It is evident that a "good cop" will always display better results as compared to a "bad cop." During an interview, a person may appear as empathetic, and they will end up gaining access to more information as compared to the person who appears cold. It is also advisable to avoid being accusatory during the interrogation process.

2. Surprising the Suspects

A deceptive individual will always try to anticipate your next move. For instance, they may try to anticipate your next question so that they can ensure each answer they are issuing seems natural. You should always ask those questions that they do not expect.

3. Listening More Than You Speak

If you are a liar, you will focus on speaking more, and your main goal is to ensure that you will sound legitimate. Also, you will focus on winning over a certain target audience. Some liars may make use of some complex sentences so that they can conceal the truth.

You should be aware of the following:
- When people are stressed, they tend to speak faster.
- A stressed person will speak louder.
- The liars usually clear their voice and cough regularly, and that means that they are experiencing some tension.

Although the statements that have been mentioned above are supposed to enlighten you on how to spot a liar, it is good to note that some people may exhibit some signs of tension, but that is not an indicator that they are lying to you. In case you have noticed any of the mentioned actions, you should proceed with caution.

4. Pay Attention to How a Person says, "No"

When engaging a suspect, you should pay close attention to how they utter the word "No." A person depicting some unusual behavior will always face another direction as they say, "No." They may also appear hesitant, and they can also close their eyes.

5. Watch for the Changes in Behavior

When a person changes their behavior, it is an indicator that they may be engaging in deceptive behavior. You should be careful when a person issues some short answers to different questions. Also, they may pretend that they are suffering from memory lapse, especially at a critical moment. They can also start to speak formally, and they may start issuing some exaggerated responses.

6. Always Ask for the Story Backward

If a person is indeed truthful, they will add some details, and they will focus on remembering more stories about what happened. A liar will start by memorizing the story, and they will stick to one narrative. If they add some details, by taking a close look at the details, you will notice that they are not adding up. If you suspect someone is deceptive, you should ask them to recall the event in a backward manner, rather than issuing the narrative from the beginning to the end. You can ask them to talk more about what happened right before a certain point. A person who is telling the truth will usually recall many details. A liar will simplify the story, and they will also contradict themselves.

7. Beware of the Compliments Issued by People

Although compliments are good, they are only good if a genuine person has issued them. You should always be on the lookout for a person who is trying to make a good impression. When you agree with all the opinions being issued by a person and also laugh at all their jokes, it is an indicator that you may be insincere.

8. Asking a Follow-Up Question

People do not like dealing with liars; however, it is good to remember that sometimes people are uneasy with some questions, since they are avoiding instances of personal embarrassment. Also, some people may be extremely dependent on the outcome of a specific conversation.

For instance, during a job interview, a person may be tempted to hide the details about why they may have been fired from their previous job. Although the person may be qualified and their personality is good, they may hide some of these details since they are in dire need of a job. During the interview, a person may issue a response that may seem puzzling. If you are puzzled during an interview by some of the responses, you can come up with some follow-up questions. If you are in doubt, you can continue to ask questions. With time, you will be able to spot whether a person is deceptive or not.

Chapter 7: What Makes a Cult? 10 Brainwashing Tell-Tale Signs

Mind control is a large discipline that covers the subject of cults as well as sects. These are small groups that use deception to control minds while applying tactics to take advantage of the vulnerability of others. These groups also apply several modern and proven tactics that may end up exposing others to danger. These methods are also applied by cult leaders to seek the attention of followers. A one-on-one cult is often defined as an intimate relationship in which an individual abuses their power to manipulate another. It could be a teacher, preacher, or government official. It could also be a therapist who seeks to extort a client. In a different case, it could also be about an abusive and controlling relationship between a couple.

Disintegrating the Cult Psychology

Cults are known for capturing people's attention based on the services and products they claim to offer in the long run. Both fascinating and terrifying, students may want to comprehend the lessons that might be garnered from these "secret" societies. The main question is usually, where does the management come from? What are some of the psychological elements of the cult? Who would live for that? To successfully answer these questions, some people have also been drawn into joining a cult.

With that said, we live in a world filled with challenges where people have abstract issues that need to be solved urgently. As such, these individuals may be vulnerable and end up trying to find various solutions. The same people may look for solutions in the wrong places. According to Dr. Adrian Furnham, who describes the issue in *Psychology Today*, humans are known to crave clarity in all forms possible. Therefore, some people are blinded by the offer of "clarity" from those who would like to take advantage of them. Cults attract people from all backgrounds and ethnicities, but often these people have one thing in common: low self-esteem. They are focused on improving their lives and are manipulated by the often simple messages of cult leaders, who promise the concrete "answers" they seek. The average person is intrigued by the whole idea of a cult and its impact on people's lives.

Many people have also successfully recruited others into their cults to maintain the life of the family tree. Generally, individuals in a cult don't look to recruit people with health issues, such as handicaps or those who are depressed. People with low self-esteem are preferred since they are vulnerable and looking for external approval and answers to make them feel good. Where possible, cults tend to take advantage of other people who are in dire need of community support when it comes to matters of physical and mental well-being. Most of the time, such individuals are compromised in one way or another. Eventually, the idea is to grow a cult's following, to extend its life and relevance. Cults generally aren't motivated to recruit the best of the world's brains, since it may be challenging to control such people.

Once people have been admitted into a cult, they are usually bombarded with love and care. This is a strategy that's commonly used on someone with low self-esteem, as they are flattered, seduced, and complimented; this trains their brain to see the cult as a source of love and acceptance. In the world today, there are many abstract issues that cause people confusion, leading some individuals to seek "concrete" answers within a cult environment. These problems need to be addressed by professional psychologists, who understand how cults are run. Cult leaders are known to promote messages that make sense at that moment in time. Beyond the scenario and in reality, such messages do not make sense. They do not contain any great content that can be substantiated.

Some research suggests that women are more likely to join a cult than men. Why, you may ask?

According to Dr. David Bromley of the prestigious Virginia Commonwealth University, women are intrigued by the fact that they can easily change their lifestyles just by joining a cult. Therefore, this makes them more statistically likely to become members of cults that will victimize them in the long run. This is also because women are more vulnerable and seduced by the appeal of gaining various advantages that have been promised, including access to education as well as funds to take care of their children. It could also be linked to the historical oppression of women. Young women who don't feel independent may sometimes be drawn to a cult; by joining they feel they are "taking charge" of their own life. To such women, it's all about seizing the opportunity and creating a better life for themselves. According to the opinion of many prominent psychologists, such as Dr. Stanley H. Cath, many of these cult members need treatment after being immersed in a cult. From his first-hand experience, it's clear that this is an interesting trend affecting masses of people in different parts of the world. Many individuals joining cults have experienced religion in their lives. They have also rejected it. Maybe this is pretty surprising to some extent, since cults are known for being religious. In the opinion of Dr. Cath, it's clear that this is a trend and a major sign of a deeper issue that needs to be addressed in society. Some of the individuals who end up joining cults are intelligent and successful in business, for example. Other than that, many people who have joined these cults are known for being exposed to emotional and physical abuse at some point in their lives.

Cults and secret societies are powerful, since they isolate members from their initial lives that were not cult-related. They break down a person's former identity and build a new one, cultivating a mentality of "us" versus "them." As such, leaders of a cult will tend to convince their victims to separate themselves from the society in which they grew up. To successfully achieve this, the cult leader is generally charming, and has to master the tactics of mind control and how to apply them for their personal gain.

Ten signs that you are in a cult include:

1. The Leader is Normally the Ultimate Authority

If you are not in a position to criticize your leader, it means that you are possibly in a cult. Charismatic leaders are the ones that form cults, and they always claim that they possess some special knowledge. In some instances, they may refer to themselves as "messiahs" or "messengers." Charismatic cult leaders may also manifest in the form of military officials, executives within a company, or even politicians. Cult leaders normally convince their members to ignore critical thinking, so they have a sense of belonging, purpose, and authority over them. Members are not allowed to question the evidence that is presented by the cult leader. The leader is always right, and they should never be questioned even when they mislead the flock. It is forbidden to criticize the leaders.

2. The Group Suppresses Skepticism

If you can only study your organization using approved sources, there is a possibility that you are in a cult. Cults usually view critical thinking as a threat, and they focus on suppressing it. If you are one of the doubting members, you will be encouraged to isolate yourself from the others so that you cannot subject them to some undue influence. You should focus mainly on the doctrines of the cult. In a cult, you are prohibited from criticizing the leaders. The members of a cult are also forbidden from consuming material that does not align with the cult's doctrines.

3. The Group Can Delegitimize Former Members

If you are finding it difficult to leave a certain group, it is an indicator that you may be part of a cult. The cult normally considers itself as the chief authority, and it does not want members to leave at any given moment. Cult leaders usually come up with false narratives that are meant to deceive members and deter them from leaving. If a member speaks out, they are perceived as bitter, evil, dishonest, and angry. Cults will shun members who go against the doctrines, to prevent them from influencing other members.

4. The Group May Be Paranoid about the Outside World

If a group starts to talk about the end of the world being near, it is an indicator that they may be part of a cult. The cult will position itself to make members believe that the evil from the outside world cannot affect them. Such cults usually thrive on conspiracy theories, persecution complexes, and catastrophic thinking. In a bid to attract more members, these cults ensure that they are aggressive while recruiting people. They can also claim that they are "saving" people from the evil that is present in the world. When a person rejects the message of the cult, they are termed as "stupid" or "evil."

5. The Group Depends Greatly on Shame Cycles

If you normally rely on your group so that you may feel loved, sufficient, or worthy, it means that you are in a cult. Cult leaders normally focus on ensuring that they have trapped their members in shame cycles. They will impose a code of conduct that is strict. They will come up with prescriptions about appearance, diet, and relationships. By members of the cult guilt-tripping other members, they position themselves as unique. When one of the members feels unworthy, they will start to talk more about their shortcomings to the cult leader. The leader will use this opportunity to further entrench their power over the member, and they will decide whether the member is worthy or not.

6. Cult Leaders Are Usually Above the Law

Cult leaders tend to assume that they are above the law, and that is why they focus more on exploiting their members sexually and economically, and there are no repercussions. When a cult leader is apprehended and confronted, they will fail to confess their wrongdoings. They will come up with justifications as to why they engage in different acts. A loyal cult member will also try to justify the behavior of their leader.

7. The Group May Use Certain Methods to Reform the Thoughts of Members

The leaders of a cult will always make use of different brainwashing techniques so that they can break down the sense of identity of each member and their ability to think straight. The members will engage in behaviors such as prayer, fasting, scripture reading, meditation, chanting, and also at times drug abuse. At the end of it all, the person will be vulnerable, and they will more easily respond to the suggestions posed by the cult leaders. These thought-terminating methods have proven to be effective, and people will then follow their leaders blindly. The cult members will also fail to analyze some of the complex issues that may come about from time to time.

8. The Group is Elitist

If the group you are in is the "solution" to different problems in the world, it means that you are part of a cult. Cults usually view themselves as enlightened, and they transform different individuals radically throughout the globe. Elitism usually creates some form of responsibility and unity, and it is centered on a united purpose. Cult leaders can also manipulate followers to take part in subservient behaviours, such as sexual favors, risky financial behavior, and free manual labor.

9. Financial Transparency Does Not Exist

If you are not allowed to know more about what happens with the money in a group, it means you are in a cult. The group may fail to disclose how the finances are being used, and that raises a red flag. Cult leaders will continue to lead their dream life, and the followers will be tasked with making financial contributions from time to time. The members will also be encouraged to contribute some money regardless of their situation.

10. The Group May Be Performing Secret Rites

In a cult, some secret teachings may exist. If you are not in a cult, you may assume that the existence of secret rites are more of a myth; however, after joining a cult, you will learn about the reality of the ceremonies and secret teachings involved. Cults utilize the secret ceremonies as a rite of passage, and it is meant to solidify the loyalty of members. The initiation takes place after a member has taken part in different tests. In some instances, the member is only required to make a financial contribution. Cult initiations are somewhat bizarre and confusing. After the rite of passage, members of the cult become more loyal, since they are now a part of the "inner circle." These members are more susceptible, especially after undergoing the rite of passage to cement their membership in a cult.

Chapter 8: Media Manipulation: Strategies and How to See Through Them

Media Manipulation

Some of the tactics and techniques that are used by various media outlets include psychological manipulation, logical fallacies, the use of rhetorical questions, the use of propaganda, and outright deception. The main focus of this kind of media organization is on suppressing the information and the points of view of the target population, while dictating what their options and thoughts should be. Some people will be forced to listen to specific one-sided arguments. People's attention may also be diverted elsewhere, away from the real issues.

Some of the media manipulation strategies that are currently in use will be discussed in this section. There is indeed a huge number of people who may not be aware of "media manipulation." Although people lack basic knowledge about what media manipulation entails, some researchers have taken the bold step to come up with a list of different techniques that are used by deceptive individuals, such as politicians and media outlets that support them, since they want to control the public.

When looking into different media manipulation techniques, the main focus is on learning more about the techniques used when carrying out mass manipulation. Media manipulation strategies work to ensure that people are submissive, docile, obedient, and don't think for themselves. Additionally, some media outlets can support inequality, capitalism, and neo-capitalism.

Some of the popular media manipulation techniques are as follows:

1. Distraction

The distraction strategy is meant to deviate the target population from focusing on the important issues that pose significance in their lives. To ensure that people are distracted, media houses can flood the news with stories that revolve around trivial issues. The main objective is to ensure that the people are distracted by making sure that their minds are occupied. The end result is that people will stop asking questions about why the media is not looking into specific issues. In the process, people will even forget the real issues.

2. Problem-Reaction-Solution

This method can be likened to how politicians try to lure voters during an election period. The population is normally tested first. The first step is to spread rumors, and an evaluation will be carried out to assess how the general population reacts. After creating a problem, the second phase involves offering a solution to the problem. The public will view the manipulators as heroes.

3. Gradualism

This is the process of manipulating people by ensuring that they have accepted some socially unjust decisions. The population is manipulated gradually. The gradual manipulation may take place for many years.

4. Differing

Another strategy used by the media is differing; this is the instance whereby people present some unpopular decisions, and they may emphasize that the decisions should be implemented since the general population will benefit significantly. The public may believe everything genuinely, and they may make some sacrifices, which they believe will bring forth some significant changes. For instance, the politicians may be the manipulators in this case, and they may trick the voters into thinking that they will lead a better life after the polls. At the end of it all, the people will realize that no changes have been implemented and they lose faith and disengage with the system.

5. Treating People like Children

The media may be focusing on manipulating the public regularly. When they manipulate the public continuously, it is an indicator that they are treating people like children. The media will try to brainwash people through the use of sugarcoated arguments, intonations, and characters. The media will, in turn, assume that people are immature, and they are incapable of handling the truth. The main goal is to ensure that the target audience is docile, submissive, and they are reacting as planned. Media manipulation ensures that people cannot think like adults.

6. Appealing to People's Emotions

The media has learned more about how to appeal to people's emotions, and their main focus is on ensuring that people are unable to think critically. Various media outlets that want to push an agenda want to control people's thoughts. You should look into how powerful fear is as a tool.

7. Keeping the Public Mediocre and Ignorant

Some media organizations prefer dealing with people who are uncultured and also ignorant. By ensuring that people are isolated from various pieces of knowledge, the media can easily manipulate the public, this is also true for certain politicians. The media also ensures that a rebellion does not take place since people are ignorant.

8. Encouraging the Public to Accept Mediocrity

By ensuring that the public accepts mediocrity, it is similar to ensuring that the general population is ignorant. The media prefers to make use of such strategies when manipulating people. For instance, is the media airing the shows that people want to watch? Are some shows imposed on us by the media? In short, do we get to consume the content that we want, or does the media impose different pieces of content on us? At times it is clear that the media is brainwashing us, and we have ceased to care much about our surroundings. Also, we have been trained to be mediocre.

9. Self-Blame

The media usually encourages self-blame and ignorance and also makes sure that people believe that they are responsible for their own misfortunes. In short, the media will focus on self-incrimination, and will make sure that the public will not mobilize at all costs.

10. Completing the Knowledge of the Public

To control the general public, the media has focused on learning more about its audience. The media can work together with other companies to learn more about every individual in an attempt to easily manipulate the masses.

It is advisable to learn more about how to spot media manipulation. The resources talking about how to spot media manipulation are few; as a result, we cannot delve into the topic in an in-depth manner. However, pay attention and you may notice now when various media outlets are trying to manipulate people.

Chapter 9: Political Propaganda: Tools, Mechanisms, and Ways to Avoid It

Political Propaganda – this is defined as people spreading false information because they support a particular cause. Propaganda is presented negatively, especially when dealing with politicians, since they often make false claims so that they can lure citizens into voting for them.

Techniques and How Political Propaganda Works

During the election period, politicians are supposed to campaign. They will talk about what they will do for the citizens. In turn, people will vote for them. After assuming office, the politicians may fail to heed their promises. People who are disappointed may vow never to vote for them again. Surprisingly, the politicians will make use of political propaganda, and commonly the people will end up voting for the same politicians.

Present political propaganda techniques have proven to be greatly effective. Nowadays, people making use of political propaganda are focusing on symbolism. When targeting the mind of a voter, you should also hit their heart. Politicians will also make use of generalizations, and they will make sure that some things sound great. On the surface, things may look good, but when you dig deeper, you will realize that the people making use of propaganda are trying to deceive all their followers.

The Tools of Propaganda

A propagandist will always make use of certain tools so that they can mobilize some followers. The most important tool is suggestion, and it aligns with stimulation. The propagandists will stimulate other people to accept all they have to say without challenging their assertions. Since stimulation is a propaganda device, it makes sure that people can accept all the propositions that are brought forth without even thinking logically.

The propagandist will make use of this tool by coming up with some positive statements that are meant to entice a group of people. They will always present their statements using a familiar language, and they will ensure that they have incorporated simplicity in each instance. By failing to admit the reality, the propagandist will be able to amass a huge following.

Suggestion is also used in the advertising sector. Another commonly used tool is insinuations, hints, and indirect statements. The best example, in this case, is the advertisement sector. One example is political advertisements, which are often pure propaganda with manipulated "facts" or outright deceptions.

Another tool is when a propagandist focuses on learning more about people, in order to know how to appeal to and manipulate his target audience

Looking into Social Media Tools

Social media ensures that people can keep in contact through the use of applications such as Facebook. For instance, there is a group of young individuals that learned about the Tinder dating app, and they began to influence their colleagues. With time, some of the conversations within the platform would be more about politics.

On various social media sites, certain propagandists send messages targeting various voters with mis-information. The users of these sites had agreed to the terms and conditions while signing up. It is not clear how many candidates manage to win elections by carrying out social media campaigns.

Nowadays, social media is among the online applications that are widely used. About 70 percent of adults in the United States have signed up on Facebook. A huge percentage of the people who have signed up on Facebook and different social media applications log into these platforms regularly. The majority of the people are also not using social media platforms for politics; they are using these platforms rather for self-expression, finding articles, and sharing content.

Social media has become common, and it is a major part of people's lives. It is also trusted, unregulated, and targetable. Since social media has attracted a considerable population, politicians were bound to make use of such tools during the election period. There is a substantial amount of evidence that social media is being used to deceive and manipulate voters.

Since technology has also advanced greatly, the news feed is also automated, and that means that the politicians may focus on manipulating different social networks. The best example, in this case, is the manner in which about half of the Twitter conversations globally usually originate from bots. Some of these accounts contain a substantial amount of political content. The political content has been well crafted, such that the targets will not realize that they are chatting with a bot.

Some of these bots have been used in other nations such as Brazil during the election period. The bots were used during the period when one of the presidents was being impeached. They came in handy when carrying out the impeachment campaign. Also, the bots were used during the mayoral race that took place in Rio. The majority of political leaders are also making use of social media tools, especially in young democracies that are utilizing automation in a bid to spread information.

Chapter 10: Psychological Warfare: Don't Be Manipulated

When it comes to manipulation, the manipulator will always focus on getting what they want, using various forms of trickery. Many people believe that manipulation is immoral. Since psychological manipulators use various deception techniques, we will look into each of these tactics and offer a suitable solution on how people can defend themselves in case of any eventuality.

Method 1 – Gaining Manipulation Skills

1. Take an Acting Class

When it comes to manipulation, it is good to learn more about how to master emotions while making sure that other people can become receptive, whenever you tend to become emotional. To learn more about expressing yourself using various techniques that play on people's emotions, it is good to enroll in an acting class. While in an acting class, it will be possible to gain some powers of persuasion. Always focus on the main goal, which involves understanding the methods of manipulating people, so you can protect yourself.

2. Enroll in a Public Speaking Class

The acting classes are meant to make sure that you can master your emotions and how you display them. The main reason why enrolling for a debate class is advisable is because you will be able to learn more about convincing other people about your argument. You will learn more about how to organize your thoughts clearly. Additionally, a public speaking class will also enlighten you about how to sound convincing. A manipulative person will use these skills to influence the actions of others by convincing them to do what they want.

3. Come up with Similarities

Manipulators always make sure that they have learned more about the body language of their target victims. They also look into the intonation patterns of their victims before they can proceed with the manipulation process. Eventually, the manipulators will come up with persuasive methods, and they will also appear calm. Watch out for this type of behavior.

4. Being Charismatic

Charismatic individuals often have a way of getting what they want. When understanding how charming people can manipulate others, you will have to ensure that you have worked on your own charisma. Not everyone who is charismatic is manipulative, so pay attention to understand who is sincere and who is misleading you. You should also be able to smile, and your body language should showcase that you are approachable, so that people feel they can easily approach you and talk to you. You must also be able to initiate a conversation with any individual, regardless of various factors, such as age. Some of the techniques that you can utilize to become charismatic include:

- Ensuring that people feel special. The best way to achieve this is through maintaining eye contact while conversing with a person. Make sure that you have also initiated a discussion about how they feel and the interests that they have. Always show the other person that you care, and you want to learn more about them. An insincere charismatic person will pretend to care about the other person, even when they don't.

- Always maintain high levels of confidence. Charismatic people are always passionate about everything that they do. It is also advisable to have confidence in yourself.

5. Learn from the Masters

If you have a friend who happens to be a psychological manipulator, you should observe them and also take notes, so you know what to look out for from potential manipulators. Always carry out a case study and ensure that the manipulators are the main point of focus. It will be possible to learn a lot from them. Pay attention to how these individuals get what they want. They may also share some insight into how they manipulate people. The main issue is that you might end up being tricked, but you will gain some insight into how to manipulate people effectively, and therefore how to avoid being manipulated.

6. Learn More about How to Read People

Each individual has a psychological and emotional makeup, and it always varies from one individual to another. When you learn about the psychological and emotional makeup of a person, it will be possible to manipulate them. People who are manipulative will often learn more about the individual that they are going to manipulate, and in many cases they become trusted by the person before they slowly take advantage of them. Some of the things that you may notice as you try to understand people include:

- Most people are vulnerable, and it is possible to reach out to them by evoking their emotional responses. For instance, some people may cry when watching a movie, and they may showcase high levels of sympathy and empathy. For a person to manipulate such individuals, they often joke around with their emotions while also pretending to feel sorry, and they will eventually get what they want by playing on the other person's emotions.

- Other people have a strong sense of guilt. Most of the individuals who have a guilt reflex grew up in a restrictive household, and they may have been punished for every wrong deed that they committed. Manipulators may make sure that the person feels guilty about various acts, so they are more likely to give in to a manipulator's demands at the end of it all.
- Some people usually respond to rational approaches. For example, if you have a close friend who is always logical and always keeps up with the news, that means that they are always after verifiable information. In such an instance, a manipulative person will make sure that they have utilized their persuasive powers accordingly when manipulating them.

Method 2 – Using Different Manipulation Techniques

1. Impose an Unreasonable Request, Then Present a Reasonable One

This is a technique that has proven to be very effective, and many manipulators often use it. It is also shockingly simple. Whenever a person wants to manipulate someone, they come up with a request that is not reasonable. The other person will reject the unreasonable request, and in that instance, a reasonable request is presented. The new request should be appealing to the individual who is being targeted. The best example to use in such a case is when an employee may not accept a permanent request to arrive early at work, but they will voluntarily accept a request whereby they are supposed to arrive at work early over a specific period of time to handle various urgent duties. The employee will prefer engaging in a short-term request, since it is less cumbersome when compared to the long-term request.

2. Inspire Fear, Then Ensure That the Victim Has a Sense of Relief

A manipulator may have chosen their victims carefully, based on who is the most vulnerable. In this case, a manipulative person will make sure that a victim's worst fears have come to life. In the process, they will then focus on ensuring that these fears are relieved, and the victim will be happy enough to give them what they want. This kind of manipulation is dangerous and you should reach out to people who can help to keep you safe from an abusive dynamic like this.

An example of how this kind of behavior might begin – assume that you have a car. Your friend might try to shock you by telling you that the car was producing some funny noises and that the engine might be dead. At that juncture, you will be in fear. After that, they inform you that they realized the strange noise was being produced by the radio. You are relieved. Since you are relieved, your friend may go ahead and ask for another favor, such as – they want to borrow the car again.

3. Ensure That a Person Feels Guilty

A manipulator may try to get what they want by invoking guilt in another person. For starters, they might carry out an evaluation and learn more about how to make someone feel guilty, by making that person feel bad for a variety of reasons.

If the manipulator is targeting their parents, for example, they would showcase that it's their parents' fault that they are the way they are in that moment.

If invoking some form of guilt among one of their friends, they may make sure that they have enlightened their friend about the number of times that they have been let down by them.

4. Bribe a Person

When a manipulative person is after something, they may issue a bribe. In such an instance, they do not have to use tactics such as blackmail to get what they want. A reward may be given but in the form of a bribe. The manipulator will learn more about your needs but will try to hide the fact that they are issuing a bribe.

5. Pretend That You Are the Victim

When a manipulative person pretends that they are a victim, they will attract some sympathy. This is a commonly used method for some people, who "play" the victim any chance they get. They usually make sure that they don't overdo the act in an attempt to get what they are looking for at the end of it all. Victims always appear helpless, and that means that the target will appear vulnerable as they offer to help them. They will pretend to be dumb, although they know what they are doing. They may pretend to be pathetic and helpless but will get more desperate and even enraged if you realize and don't give in to this type of emotional manipulation. You need to try to discern who is a real victim and who is manipulating you.

6. Use Logic

Logic is important in some of the day to day activities that you engage in. Always ensure that you have come up with a list of reasons as to why you would benefit from the things that you are asking for from someone. A manipulative person will always present their case, calmly and rationally, but they will make sure to display some emotions, to get what they want at the end of it all.

7. Maintain the Character

Depending on the method that has been used, a manipulator will try to make sure that they have displayed some emotions that could relate to their current scenario.

They may appear worried or even upset, depending on the matter at hand.

Method 3 – Manipulate Anyone in Your Life

As a manipulator, a person may develop different tendencies, including manipulating other people who are close to them in real life.

1. Manipulating Your Friends

When it comes to manipulating or being manipulated by your friends, you might realize that it is a tricky situation. Perhaps your friend has been making sure to flatter you, always making sure that they have been nice while also doing some small favors, in case they need a favor within a few days. If someone is a "real" friend they won't need to manipulate you for a favor, and vice versa. Try to stay away from toxic "friends." Some ways that the manipulation may be carried out:

- Utilize your emotions – your friends should be caring individuals; as a result, they will not want to see you upset. If you have any acting skills, make sure that you have used them accordingly to ensure that you will appear to be a very upset individual.

- Constantly remind your friend about how good they are – always ensure that you remember the periods when you have always done some good things for the sake of your friend.

- Guilt-trip your friends – you do not have to utilize the "bad friend" card. Always mention someone casually and remind them about how they have let you down. Always make it sound like your friend is uncaring without going overboard.

2. Manipulating Your Significant Other

If you have a manipulative partner, they may attempt to gain favors by turning you on and asking for the favor, so you understand you cannot get what you want unless you heed their demands. They may try "buttering you up" by asking for favors after giving you compliments or lightening the mood. These examples are the kind of thing that might happen, before more damaging behavior escalates. You should try not to get too deeply involved with a romantic partner who is manipulative as it is possible they will be abusive in other ways.

3. The Impression You Use Determines Whether Your Manipulation Techniques Will Subdue the Target

A manipulative person will always make sure that they are deceptive and also swift. What matters most to them is ensuring that their image is still intact.

- Utilize emotions – look into what your significant other would do when they realize that you are wallowing in sorrow. In most cases, your partner will ensure that they have reignited the happiness within you.
- Public embarrassment – if your partner is determined to solicit a favor from you, they may have utilized the waterworks approach in a public place. The best example to showcase the effectiveness of such an approach is – when a child tries to solicit a favor from their parents in public, the child hopes the parent will give in to their demands. This technique will most likely be used sparingly.
- Issue small bribes – to encourage a favor, such as going out on a dinner date or to any other event, small bribes might be used.

4. Manipulating Your Boss

When dealing with professional relationships, for example in an employee / manager dynamic, there are some things that can be done to increase the chance of a positive working relationship and of you being able to appropriately appeal to your boss for what you want from time to time. Use the approaches that are logical and rational when dealing with your boss. When you have some personal problems, do not discuss them in front of your boss. Also, do not appear at your boss's desk crying because of some personal issues. There is a high chance that you will be fired. When dealing with your boss, make sure that you are logical. Also, make sure that you have provided some good reasons regarding why you need some assistance from your boss.

- Make sure that you are a model worker. Such a technique will always work when you need to make a request. Also, make sure that you are working a bit late. Additionally, make sure that you are always happy and smiling whenever you are around your boss.
- When soliciting a favor from your boss, make sure that you have done so in an offhand manner. Always request casually. For instance, approach your boss in the office and tell them that there is an important matter that you wanted to discuss with them. When your boss hears that, they will issue you their undivided attention, and they will enact on your favor at the end of the day.
- Try to ask for a favor at the end of the day. Do not engage your boss early in the morning. First, make sure that you have observed their mood. If they showcase that they are stressed, you could opt for another moment. If you want to approach your boss during a break, you can do so as they go to look for lunch. They will want to quickly deal with your requests, and they will not also argue with you.

5. Manipulating the Teacher

If you want to manipulate your teacher, you must do so professionally. Also, make sure that you have incorporated some emotions. During the specific day that you want to make a request, you should make sure that you have appeared before the teacher as a model student. Also, make sure that you have arrived in class early. Try to ensure that the teacher can notice that you have been reading a lot. In short, the teacher should note that you are taking your studies seriously. While in the classroom, make sure that you are active, and you should be focused.

- Always enlighten the teacher about how great they are, and you should do so casually. Tell them about how they inspire you. In some instances, also ensure that you have enlightened them about how much you love the subjects that they are teaching.

- Mention some stuff about what is happening at home. Although the situation might appear to be awkward, the teacher will be able to sympathize with you since they will feel sorry, and they might want to learn more about your situation.

- As you discuss your personal life, ensure that you have done so in a strategic manner, and your teacher will eventually become uncomfortable. If you had delayed when it comes to issuing your assignment, the teacher might have some pity on you because of your situation, and they will offer you an extension, which means you can submit your assignment later. If the teacher refuses to grant you an extension, always enlighten them that you understand that they do not extend the period when the students should hand in their assignments. Your voice should appear to be frail since you want the teacher to sympathize with you. There is a high chance that the teacher will give in to your demands.

- If such a technique does not work, you can choose to cry, since you must demonstrate that you are indeed emotional. You will start crying, and the teacher will become uncomfortable, and that means that they will be more likely to heed to your commands.

6. Manipulating Your Parents

It is evident that your parents should always love you, unconditionally. As a result, they may be more susceptible to manipulation techniques. The main fact here is that your parents love you, and they will always support you in every way possible. You have to ensure that you are a model offspring for some time before you can make a request involving certain favors. Always make sure that you have not missed your curfew. Also, make sure that you have spent most of your time studying and assisting in handling some house chores. Afterward, you can go ahead and request a favor.

- Ensure that your request is reasonable. For instance, you may want to attend a concert and the following day you should be attending school. When making such a request, make sure that you have done so casually. Always make sure that your parents can see the possibility in the situation, and they will not reject the proposal in the long run.
- You can also pose a question to your parents while you are folding laundry. When handling such tasks, your parents will remember that they have a great son or a daughter, and they will be more likely to comply with your wishes.
- Talk more about how you will engage in some of these activities together with your friends. When your parents hear that you will be engaging in a specific activity together with your friends, they will be more inclined to issue you the go-ahead to proceed.
- Ensure that your parents feel guilty. For instance, you may have wanted to go to a concert. If your parents deny you the opportunity to take part in such an event, you will just tell them that it's okay. Always make sure that your parents will feel guilty since you may be missing out on an opportunity to take part in a major event.

How to Defend Yourself from Manipulative Individuals

For starters, it is good to note that it is not possible to defend yourself from a manipulative individual. The best thing that you can do in this case is to make sure that you have first identified that the individual is indeed manipulative. If they happen to showcase that they are deceptive, you should ensure that you have kept a safe distance from these individuals. If they are not deceptive, you can continue being friends. It is also good to note that some people may mislead others by spreading false information. For example, you may come across some people talking about how manipulative a certain person is, but they are the ones trying to manipulate you and your opinion of this other person.

Never issue the manipulative person a warning. If you notice early on, you should just leave and continue leading your life as usual. After leaving them, they will look for other individuals who they can manipulate into ensuring that they have heeded their demands. If a person is unwell, you should go ahead and try to find out more about their condition. Since some people do lie, you can also go ahead and seek some expert advice from a psychologist or even a psychiatrist. If the person is unwell and they do not showcase any signs of improvement, you can move on and continue living your life as usual, if they are not threatening you.

If the manipulative individual is related to you, you should always be direct with them. Ensure that you have set some boundaries and always be firm so that they cannot dare to cross the set boundaries. Manipulative individuals will realize that they will be held accountable once they tend to showcase undesirable behaviors. How such people behave toward you will also determine how you interact with them.

If they understand some of the rules that you have set, they will in some cases be okay with that, and they will not intrude in any way. Also, ensure that you have initiated a discussion with the manipulative individual while also trying to learn more about their character and condition. Ensure that you have not lectured them in any way. Always ask questions that will help you to learn more about how they are. Never try to fix them, leave such matters to professionals such as psychiatrists or psychologists. Always ensure that you have issued them a referral to a renowned psychiatrist or any other medical practitioner who can deal with their condition accordingly. The manipulative individuals should also be issued the support that they need.

Although some of the stories issued by the manipulative individuals will appear far-fetched, you should never judge them. According to them, their story is valid, although it may appear to be made up to some extent. Ensure that you have not told them any of your stories.

If anything goes wrong, they will always use the information that they have about you to fight back. Always remember that we never choose our family members; as a result, you should choose whether you will help them or ignore them. If any other people may appear to be toxic in your life, you should also avoid them. Manipulation and abuse in romantic and other close relationships can build up with "small" occurrences, and they can end with an attempt at total control of one person over another. This is very dangerous and damaging, and you must be on alert in the early stages of manipulative behavior, to be able to get free of this kind of dynamic before it becomes totally destructive. Always seek help if you feel you need it, to stay safe from a threatening and abusive individual, as some situations escalate to an unsafe level.

How to Know If You are Being Manipulated and How to Defend Yourself

Psychological manipulation usually breeds some form of healthy social influence, and it usually occurs between many individuals. The relationships, in this case, are usually give or take. In psychological manipulation, one person will always benefit from the other by taking advantage of them. The individual manipulating the other always does it deliberately, and they often bring about an imbalance of power since they are exploiting other people for their own self-benefit.

The characteristics of manipulative individuals are;
- They know how to detect the weaknesses of other people.
- Once they identify a person's weaknesses, they will always use these weaknesses against them.
- They will always convince the victims to give up something so that they may serve their self-centered interests.
- Once a manipulative individual manages to take advantage of another person, they will always violate the other party until the exploited person ensures that the manipulation spree has come to an end.

Some of the causes of chronic manipulation are always deep-seated and complex. However, it is not easy to identify the main drive that causes a person to be manipulative psychologically. Also, when a person is being manipulated, they do encounter different challenges. The main question that arises, in this case, is how people manage such a situation. Some of the best ways to handle manipulative individuals include:

1. **Make Sure You Are Conversant with Your Human Rights**

When dealing with a psychologically manipulative individual, make sure that you know more about your human rights. It would be easy to recognize when any of your rights are being violated. Also, make sure that you are not harming other individuals. Every person has a right to stand up for themselves, while also defending each of their rights. If you harm other people, you may be violating each of these human rights. Some of the important rights include:

- The right to be treated with respect.
- The right to express opinions, feelings, and wants.
- The right to set your own priorities.
- The right to say "no" without feeling guilty.
- The right to get anything that you pay for.
- The right to have a different opinion from that of your colleagues.
- The right to protect yourself from being mistreated mentally, physically, or emotionally.
- The right to always create your own happiness while also living a healthy life.

All these human rights are meant to represent a boundary that should never be crossed by the manipulative individuals.

It is evident that our society has many people who do not respect the rights of others. Some of these psychological manipulators always want to exploit people's rights so that they may take advantage of them in every way possible. The main important thing to note is that we all have the right to declare that *we* have the power over ourselves, since most people might assume that the manipulator is the one with the power. The manipulative individual does not have any power over you whatsoever.

2. Keep Your Distance

One of the most effective ways to identify a person who is a manipulator is by observing how various individuals behave when they are around you and when they are around other individuals. If the individual happens to behave differently when they are around different people, this is a character trait that symbolizes they might be manipulative. Everyone has a degree of social differentiation, and some psychological manipulators may prove to be extreme in different instances. Or they may be polite to various individuals while being extremely rude to others. They may also seem helpless, and in other instances, they will showcase some aggressiveness. When you observe such character traits regularly, you should always keep your distance. Avoid engaging such people unless you are forced to depending on the circumstances. It was earlier mentioned that it is difficult to learn more about why people tend to be psychologically manipulative. As a result, ensure that you have kept your distance since such individuals cannot be saved from their current predicaments.

3. Avoid Self-Blame and Personalization

In most cases, manipulative individuals tend to look for a person's weakness, and they will start exploiting them afterward. The people who are being exploited may feel inadequate, and they may also indulge in some self-blame since they may have failed to satisfy the manipulator in different ways. In some of these situations, it is good to note that although you are being manipulated, you are not the problem. The manipulator is taking advantage of you while also ensuring that you feel bad about yourself. You may surrender all your rights and power to the manipulative individuals. Always ask yourself questions such as:

- Are you being treated with the respect that you deserve?
- Are the demands of the manipulative person reasonable?

- Is the relationship beneficial to one party or both parties?
- Do you feel good about the relationship?

4. Focus on Asking Probing Questions

Psychological manipulators will always issue demands to each of the individuals that they are manipulating. Some of the "offers" that they put across will seem unreasonable to some extent, but they will expect you to meet all their needs. Whenever you feel like you are being solicited unreasonably, it is good to focus on yourself by also asking the manipulator different probing questions. To look into whether each of these individuals has some self-awareness, they will recognize the inequity that is present in each of their schemes. Some of the suitable probing questions include:

- Is the relationship reasonable?
- Does what the manipulator want seem fair?
- Do you have a say in the relationship?
- Are you gaining anything?
- What are your expectations?

When you ask yourself some of these questions, you will be coming up with a mirror that is meant to show you the reality. The questions are meant to ensure that the manipulator can see the reality about their nature. In an instance whereby the manipulator has some form of self-awareness, they will withdraw the demands that they have been putting across, and they will back down. Some pathological manipulators can also be termed as narcissists, and they will dismiss each of the questions being directed to them. They will always insist you are getting in their way. If you ever find yourself in such a scenario, always ensure that you have applied different ideas that will ensure you have outsmarted the manipulative individuals. By being creative, you can hopefully bring an end to the manipulation spree.

5. Utilize Time to Your Advantage

Besides making some unreasonable requests, the manipulator will always ask questions and expect an immediate answer in each case. They will always exert some undue pressure while also striving to control the situation. The best example is people who are engaging in sales. Their main aim is to ensure that they have marketed different products successfully, and they may be manipulative so that people may purchase each of the products that they are selling. In such an instance, the manipulative individual will expect you to answer each of their questions immediately. They will also take advantage in different ways while also distancing themselves from the immediate influence that they have brought forth. Always exercise some sense of leadership by telling the manipulative individual that you will think about it and issue them an answer at an opportune moment.

Some of these words always prove to be powerful, and since we have used an example of sales agents, the customer, in this case, is the one who is supposed to address the salesperson and tell them that they will think about it. Always take time to think about the merits and demerits that may be present, depending on the current situation. Also, try to look into whether it is possible to come up with an equitable arrangement, or you should say no, depending on the current scenario.

6. Always Learn to Say "No"

It is not easy to say "no," however, you should first learn the art of communication. When you effectively learn to say "no," you will be able to stand your ground while also making sure that you have been able to maintain a workable relationship. Also, make sure that you are conversant with your human rights, most importantly the area that involves making sure that you can set your own priorities without incurring any form of guilt. After all, you have the right to choose your own happiness and a healthy life too. Always make sure that you can resist while keeping your peace.

7. Always Confront the Bullies

A psychological manipulator tends to become a bully at some point. They will always intimidate or harm their victims. The most important point to note is that the bullies will always prey on the individuals that they may perceive as weak. The manipulative individuals will go ahead with the exploitation whenever they come across an individual who is compliant and passive. When you make yourself a worthy target, the manipulative individuals will not hesitate to pounce on you. It is also evident that a majority of the people who enjoy bullying are also cowards. Whenever a person begins to showcase that they know their rights, the bullies will always back down. Various studies have also been carried out, and it is evident that most of the bullies have also been victims of violence at some point in their lives. Although the bullies have also been victimized at some point in their lives, it is not an excuse as to why they are bullying others. Such information is meant to ensure that you can view bullies from a different perspective.

When you confront a bully, you will be confident enough that you can protect yourself against various forms of danger. You may stand tall as an individual while also supporting other individuals when they are bullied. In an instance whereby a person has been psychologically, emotionally, or verbally assaulted, always make sure that you have sought the services of a counselor and also report the matters to the legal authorities, and they will take the necessary course of action. Always make sure that you can stand up to the bullies, and you may partner with some individuals who are fed up with practices such as bullying.

8. Set Consequences

When an individual who thrives on manipulation insists on violating your personal boundaries, always make sure that you are in a position to tell them "no." Always make sure that you are in a position to assert and also identify consequences. Possession of such knowledge can ensure that you can handle difficult people. When a bully understands the consequences that may come about as a result of their actions, always make sure that they can learn more about the value of respect.

Chapter 11: Workspace Manipulators: Spot Them and Stop Them

Deception Tactics at the Workplace – How to Influence People

Influencing tactics can be grouped into three categories; these are emotional, logical, or cooperative appeals. In simpler terms, it is influencing the head, heart, or hands.

- ❖ **Logical Appeal** – this is tapping into people's rational and intellectual sides. In this category, you will present your argument for the best course of action basing it on organizational or personal benefits, or both, which is appealing to people's minds.

- ❖ **Emotional Appeal** – this connects your message, goal, or project to individual goals and values. This can be by outlining ideas that promote one's feelings of well-being, service, or to achieve a sense of belonging, which tugs at the heart; hence, the chances are that it will gain much-needed support from the rest of the team.

❖ **Cooperative Appeals** – this can be translated to mean "collaboration," which is, *what are those tasks that you will do together?* While consultation involves the *ideas* that other people have, it's important to build alliances with those who have already given their support to you or who have much-needed credibility. That is why coming together for a common purpose in an organization can work wonders, because extending a hand to others can be a very effective tool when it comes to influencing.

Note that in any organization or any other place for that matter, leaders who can master these influencing skills and effectively use them can achieve their goals and objectives more successfully and amicably than leaders who lack these skills, irrespective of their management positions in that particular organization.

Which Influence Tactic Is Right for You?

You should consider the following tactics below when choosing the influence that will work best for you:

✔ **Know Your Audience.** Identify and understand each of your stakeholders. This is because each has his/her own agenda and set of special concerns and issues, perspectives, and priorities. Moreover, different groups and individuals will need different strategies for influencing. It will be very important to customize your influencing tactic for each person, with individual personalities, goals, and objectives, including organizational roles and responsibilities, in mind.

✔ **Assess the Situation.** The fundamental questions that you should first ask yourself are: *Why am I involved in this work area? Why am I in need of this other person's input? What kind of results am I trying to achieve by influencing this person?* One of the most important things to remember in this category is that you should be very clear about whom you need to influence and your set targets.

✔ **Review Your Ability.** Which tactics do you use occasionally? Which ones are most effective when used? Are there any new tactics that could be used in this situation? Can you also be inspired by others for advice or coaching? For example, if you are always focusing on making logical appeals to colleagues, then it is prudent that you have a co-worker who is a very dedicated collaborator to help you put forth your collaboration tactics and arguments.

✔ **Brainstorm Your Approach.** What are the tactics that best work for you? Which logical appeals do you think are most effective when used? How do you make either an emotional or a cooperative appeal? What exactly would you say or do in each tactic? You need to anticipate possible responses so that you adequately prepare your reply. Do you have any counterarguments that you could use? Are there any additional influencing tactics to help you through?

When starting out as a leader or in a management position, at first, it would be vital for you to try out new influencing tactics in low-risk situations, by practicing one-on-one. Then as you grow more versatile and experienced, you will gain enough confidence in your abilities in influencing other teams and larger groups. Through this experience, you will be able to persuade others in higher-stakes situations easily.

Find the approach that works best for you.

Grow Your Core Leadership Skills for Every Role

To be effective as a leader, there is a great need for you to continue developing, adapting, and strengthening your skills throughout your career. As you also gain skill in one area, you will find that there is more to be learned and practiced when moving on to new challenges and frontiers, taking on larger roles. If, as a leader, you feel that you have skipped any of the above fundamental core leadership skills in your career, then there is no need to feel inadequate that you will not be as effective as you want or that you can't fully develop your leadership skills. On the contrary, with concerted effort, you can always learn and improve skills that you missed out on. Moreover, if you can identify gaps or weaknesses in your leadership skills, then this positive mentality will enable you to have the potential to learn, grow, and change for the better. Thus, through self-awareness, communication, influence, and learning agility as the core of your leadership development and values, you can rest assured that you are setting yourself up for new opportunities and into new levels of responsibility, this is because these four core leadership skills are needed for everyone and in every stage of your career.

Dale Carnegie, in his book called *How to Win Friends and Influence People*, describes how to influence others positively and maintain great friendship as a result. Even though this book was written in 1936, these principles and lessons have stood the test of time and are always a point of reference for many influential leaders today. What stands out about these principles is that they are not about trends or fads, but are the building blocks of social intelligence, and how the practice of good social skills can improve your life.

Below are the ten best classic lessons and principles we learn from Carnegie:

1. Do Not Criticize, Condemn, or Complain

A quote from the book says, "Any fool can criticize, condemn or complain—and most fools do." Carnegie goes on to say that it takes great amounts of character and self-control to forgive for the wrongs done to you. This discipline will bring you great dividends and joy in the manner in which you relate to other people.

2. Be Generous with Praise

Carnegie recommends using praise generously in relationships, quoting Charles M. Schwab, who said:

> "In my wide association in life, meeting with many and great people in various parts of the world, I am yet to find the person,

however great or exalted in their station, who did not do better work and put forth greater effort under a spirit of approval than they would ever do under a spirit of criticism."

3. Remember People's Names

It is very difficult at times to remember people's names when you meet them for the first time, especially when you meet many people casually. However, it is possible if you train yourself in remembering names. This will make people feel very special, appreciated, and important. Carnegie goes on to say that, "Remember that a person's name is the most important and sweetest sound in any language."

4. Be Genuinely Interested in Others

Remembering people's names, and asking them questions, which will encourage them to talk freely about themselves and their interests, will eventually make people believe that you like them. They will, in turn, like you. Carnegie continues to write. "You can make more friends in two months by becoming interested in other people than you can in two years by trying to get other people interested in you." It is important for you to listen 75% and only speak 25% at all times.

5. Know the Value of Charm

People normally do not discuss the fact that when it comes to looking for jobs, getting an opportunity is not about talent, which college you attended, or who do you know, it is all about people liking you. A good resume may get you an interview, but it is your charisma, social skills, and talent that will make people want to keep you around. This is the reason why people will always pick someone whom they enjoy being around over someone they don't, no matter how talented he/she is. This has the potential to enrich your life and will, in turn, open as many doors as you ever imagined possible.

6. Be Quick to Acknowledge Your Own Mistakes

Humility beats all else. It softens even the hardest of hearts. Being humble will make people less defensive and more agreeable than when you are humble and reasonable at the same time but not enough to take responsibility for your own mistakes. It is very important to have a strong and stable personal and professional relationship with others. This will greatly hinge on you being responsible for your actions, especially when it comes to your mistakes.

7. Don't Attempt to "Win" an Argument

Carnegie writes that the best manner to win an argument is to avoid it, citing the adage: "A man convinced against his will, will still have the same opinion." Even if you can completely dismantle the other party's argument with factual information, it will not change their mind.

8. Begin on Common Ground

In the event of a disagreement, it is very prudent for both of you to start on common ground, which will make it very easy for the two of you to transition into the difficult subjects. If you start from polarizing positions, you stand to lose in a big way and might never recover lost ground even on the subjects that you originally agreed upon.

9. Have Others Believe Your Conclusion Is Their Own

You cannot force people to believe anything that they are told. This is why those people who are persuasive greatly understand how suggestion has tremendous power. You need to learn how to plant a seed, instead of telling people they are wrong, and look for common ground, so you can then easily persuade them that what they want is actually your (unspoken) desired outcome.

10. Make People Feel Important

You can achieve this without much effort: it does not cost you anything to smile; know people's names; praise them; and make an effort to learn their interests and really listen to them when they talk. All of these details can make people feel important.

Hack Others' Mind with Cognitive Biases

We human beings tend to believe that we are rational and logical in our undertakings. However, unbeknown to us, we are constantly under the influence of cognitive biases that influence our thinking, beliefs, and every other decision and judgment that we make daily.

At times, these biases can be very obvious to the discerning, and one might even recognize these predispositions while they are so hidden that they are not easy to notice.

Below are some of these cognitive biases that have a profound influence on the way we live our daily lives:

The Confirmation Bias

This type of bias is based on how people tend to listen more to information that reaffirms what they already know or believe.

The Hindsight Bias

This type of bias involves the tendency to see previous events, whether random or not, as being more predictable than they actually were.

The Anchoring Bias

As human beings, we always tend to gravitate toward the first piece of information that we receive. This is what is called the anchoring bias or anchoring effect.

The Misinformation Effect

We can be greatly influenced by memories of particular events in our lives. This involves conflating things that actually occurred after a specific event, as having occurred during the event itself. This is what we refer to as the misinformation effect.

The False-Consensus Effect

People tend to overestimate how much other people might agree with their own beliefs, behaviors, attitudes, and values. Thus, this inclination is what is known as the false consensus effect. This can, at times, make a person overvalue their views.

What is the Barnum Effect?

The "Barnum Effect" is also known as the "Forer Effect" in the field of psychology. It is a phenomenon that tends to occur when people believe that general descriptions of personalities are applied specifically to them. Therefore, this effect means that people can be gullible, due to their thinking that information is about them only, when really it is generic. The name of this effect was inspired by the phrase "There's a sucker born every minute," which has mostly been attributed to showman P.T. Barnum (though there is no evidence that he said it).

What is a "Barnum" statement?

How to Use Barnum Statements to Influence People

Astrologists, who use horoscopes, magicians, palm readers, and psychics gazing at crystal balls, make extensive use of the Barnum Effect, by convincing people that their often generic descriptions of them are highly specialized and unique; hence, they cannot apply to anyone else.

Barnum Statements are positive statements that most people will agree on, in regard to themselves. They might not be aware that almost every other person will also see themselves in the statements, and they are not, in fact, personalized.

PART 3: Unlocking Your Powers

Chapter 12: NLP: Master Persuasion & Negotiation Techniques

There is a strong relationship between Neuro-Linguistic Programming (NLP) and persuasion and influence. For starters, Neuro-Linguistic Programming involves studying the subjective human experience. It involves studying how people can create some meaning within the mind. According to some individuals, Neuro-Linguistic Programming involves studying superior thinking. Human beings usually create a sense of meaning both externally and internally. It is also possible to learn more about how people express themselves through spoken language and how they can be influenced. Language can be used to persuade people and it is an instrument that can be used to transmit internal experiences.

State Control

When it comes to influencing and persuading people, the first thing that you need to consider is whether you have a close relationship with the person. If a personal relationship does not exist, it would be difficult to persuade or influence someone. On the other hand, it is possible to create a personal relationship with someone using Neuro-Linguistic Programming. "State control" should always come about before you can focus on ensuring that you have developed a personal relationship.

NLP also allows you to learn more about how you can control your state. If you can form a close relationship with someone and observe how you feel when they are in a bad mood, for example, you should be able to gauge the feeling that you have. There are some instances whereby people feel energetic. State control is defined as the ability to link various sequences of emotional states at any given moment. It is possible to learn these techniques through Neuro-Linguistic Programming.

It is also good to note that if you are not in the right state, you cannot easily form a close relationship with someone, regardless of whether you have an in-depth understanding of Neuro-Linguistic Programming. When forming a close relationship with a person, you should ensure that your psycho-emotional state matches that of the other party. After studying Neuro-Linguistic Programming, you will be able to learn various mechanical techniques including;

> Using the verbs being used by other parties.
> Being able to match breathing patterns.
> Using the tonalities used by the other party.
> Matching their way of blinking.
> Using the posture they normally use.

After learning about Neuro-Linguistic Programming, it is possible to take your own physiology and to make sure that it matches that of the other person. It is also good to note that a close relationship cannot be formed if you are not close to the other person. The main point to note is that the NLP techniques allow people to speed up the process of becoming close to someone, while also ensuring that their frequency aligns with that of the other person, within a short period.

Classical Neuro-Linguistic Programming allows you to assume the character of the other party easily and fully, and you can easily persuade and influence them. It is also possible to fully mimic the individual. Such an eventuality is known as "pacing." Pacing involves imitating someone or talking about some things that may be true, depending on a specific experience.

You may want to form a close relationship with someone who is in a negative state, and you may not know how to go about it. If you want to form a bond with a person who is in a negative state, you won't want to be in the same negative state as them. Such consideration comes about since you must be in the same state as the other person you want to form a rapport with. Some of the phenomena that comes into play includes the presence of mirror neurons; these neurons can help you to form a desired connection with the other party.

It is also possible to change someone's state. When approaching someone, you must first observe the environment. You may have different options, and they include interrupting the other person. Most people lack the courage to interrupt a person. The other option involves ensuring that you can match the other person's state. By changing their state to your own, you can easily change the state of the other individual.

When you approach a person and depict high energy levels, there might be a huge difference in the frequency of the two parties, and you may fail to relate. For instance, your energy levels may be higher than that of the target individual, and that means that your states cannot align. Also, some states cannot be easily interrupted. The moment when you form a connection with someone and your frequencies do not align, it is still possible that you will relate.

What are the Fundamentals of Human Behavior and Change?

Events such as modeling, action, and effective communication are some of the key components of Neuro-Linguistic Programming. The belief here is that if an individual can understand how the other party accomplishes a task, then the overall process can easily be copied and communicated to others at the same time for them to also complete the task at hand.

Proponents of this concept opine that everyone has a personal map of reality. Therefore, those who practice NLP normally analyze their own idea of reality, and any other perspectives, to come up with a workable and systematic overview of a situation. By understanding a wide range of perspectives, these NLP users gain considerable amounts of information. Those advocating for this concept believe that our senses play a vital role when it comes to processing the available information and that our bodies and mind can influence one another. Hence, Neuro-Linguistic Programming is an experiential approach to all this, and for anyone to understand an action, then surely they must perform that same action if they are to learn from the experience.

Moreover, NLP practitioners have this belief that there are natural hierarchies when it comes to learning, communicating, and change. The six logical levels of change are listed below:

Spirituality and Purpose – this can be termed as involvement in something that might be larger than life. It could be involvement in matters of religion, ethics, or any other system. This presents one of the highest levels of change.

Identity – this normally involves how you view yourself. It can also include the responsibilities and other roles in your life.

Beliefs and Values – This system entails all your personal beliefs, including all the issues that matter in every aspect of your life.

Capabilities and Skills – This category involves all your abilities and what you can accomplish by using them.

Behaviors – These are the specific actions, which you can perform.

Environment – This is your setting, including where you live. It also includes the people around you. Normally, this is seen as the lowest level of change one can effect.

The purpose of each of these logical levels in our lives is to organize and direct any flow of information. Therefore, when it comes to making any change in the lower tier, it can also have an overall effect on the higher levels. The same theory also applies to changes in the higher levels, according to NLP practitioners.

How to Safeguard Yourself from Manipulation/Persuasion

All our emotions, whether good or bad, have a certain purpose in our lives. However, you should be on the lookout for those who want to exploit you for their own personal gains by using the mighty power of emotions. Any time you feel emotionally drained, it is important for you to go through these tips below for the protection of your very own energy field against external exploitation.

1. Don't Fall into Their Trap

In this world, some people take great pleasure in exploiting other people's emotions and will use every trick in the book to their advantage. These are elements that include confusion, blame games, and interrogation, to get the better of you. You need to find ways of effectively dealing with them. You can achieve this by ignoring them or politely refusing their advances, as opposed to meeting them.

2. Start Writing Down What They Say During Conversations

While this might be a bit awkward, emotional manipulators tend to make you look bad. The trick is to twist their words to fit their motive. If you are not careful, you may even start to take their word for it and believe what they say. To ensure that it does not happen, you can replay the things they said in previous conversations by writing down every detail you might feel is important in countering them.

3. Steer Clear Whenever Possible

Just steer clear of these types of people. This is because emotional manipulators are very clever people who will stop at nothing to take advantage of you and will render slim any chance of you taking advantage of them.

4. Call Them out on Their Behavior

These people know how the human mind works, simply because they have probably been able to boss people around and they have never been caught out or held accountable for their actions. Therefore, when confronted by these con artists, you must stand up for yourself. Let it be known that you do not condone any form of nonsense from them.

5. Avoid Emotional Attachment with Them

I know this might be easier said than done. This is especially so when they do not initially show their true identity. However, as a potential victim, you should pay close attention to the first signs that might indicate they are about to open up your emotional roller coaster. Slowly but surely, back away from this toxic relationship for your own benefit. Make sure that you make them know your boundaries. One thing that emotional manipulators are good at is that they are constantly on the lookout for their next prey. However, it would be easier for you to break away if you have not invested much emotionally in this relationship.

6. Meditate Often

For you not to be caught off-guard, you must always keep a positive mindset through constant meditation, by keeping your mind silent, deep breaths, if possible get in touch with the higher realms to adequately handle yourself down here on Earth. This will come in handy when dealing with emotional manipulators, in the best manner possible. This is because you are assured of inner peace no matter the amount of chaos that surrounds you; you will have great composure within yourself. Meditations of love and kindness will enable you to look at such a person in a different light, enabling you to develop compassion for them. It may even open your eyes to see the possibilities of what they have gone through in their lives for them to be the way they are. You will always have peace of mind when you practice the art of meeting hostility with love and understanding. You never know that it is such gestures that may transform an emotional manipulator into a new being after all.

7. Inspire Them

In this regard, you need to be the agent of change. This will position you at a great advantage because it will inadvertently shield you from any negative sentiments that may be thrown at you by emotional manipulators after your own non-manipulative and positive countermeasures have inspired them. If need be, to stall them in their tracks, bring out the benefits that come with meditating, and the simple ways in which they can take responsibility for their own actions and lives, among other life's positive attributes.

8. Tell Them, "You're Right"

As hard as it might seem for your ego, you will always have peace of mind, and your soul will always rest easy knowing that you are composed and cannot be taken advantage of by these parasites. Emotional manipulators always thrive on drama, and the better if you agree with them on anything they say. This, in turn, will leave them clueless, quickly extinguishing any hope that they had of exploiting your emotions. This is because, for the sake of your emotional wellbeing and peace of mind, you just let them have their way in the argument. However, deep within yourself, you darn well know that everything being said about you is false.

9. Let Go of Harmful Relationships

If you realize that either your boyfriend or girlfriend has the tendency to be emotionally manipulative, then the best thing for you is to leave the relationship early enough while your dignity and self-worth are still high. This is for your own good and peace of mind. You can never impose change on anyone who is like this, no matter the countless times that you have brought forth their violent behavior or put up with them. Someone of your caliber deserves someone who will nurture and take good care of you and your emotional well-being, and not someone who wants to take advantage of you for their own selfish motives.

10. Develop a Strong Mentality

You should never let another person's insults and outbursts get the better of you. Remember, this is just a ploy to get under your skin. Instead, the best thing you could do for yourself is to find humor in these insults. Another trick you could do is entertaining their sentiments without seemingly agreeing with them. If you have an unshakable and strong sense of self-esteem, then nothing they say will get into your head.

11. Give Yourself Positive Self-Talk Throughout the Day

Masters of emotional manipulation can destroy your image and mood. Ensure that you can restore everything by uplifting yourself to greater heights where nobody can pluck them. This is because they thrive best when they see you battered and bruised emotionally. That is when they swoop in for the kill. However, when they see that you are unperturbed by their advances, they will leave you alone; hence, they will not have any valid reason to get closer to you any longer.

Some other suitable negotiation techniques:

Frame the Negotiation as a Collaboration, and it Will Be Used to Solve a Common Problem

The most important factor to note is that the main focus should be on the opponent since they are the main problem. You should not come up with a "me" vs. "them" mentality. Also, your choice of words and body language should not showcase that you are bringing about some competitiveness. The first step should entail establishing your goals. After you come up with your objectives, you can work with a more general purpose.

No Immediate Retort

This is an important skill that you should possess so that you can handle a negotiation effectively. After a person comes up with an idea, you should not come up with a counter-argument immediately. First, share the ideas that you have. After that, the person who came up with the idea will be more interested in hearing what you have to say. Do not try to pin your idea fast. Ensure that you have discussed the initial idea accordingly. You can also come up with some questions and explore the proposal that has been brought forth. After some time, the other party will start to address any concerns that you may have.

Chapter 13: The Antidote to Groupthink: 10 Ways to Beat the Herd

Groupthink – this is a term used to describe what takes place when a group of people comes together, and their main desire is to maintain harmony within the group at any cost. The desire to maintain cohesiveness brings about a tendency whereby all the members come to a consensus without arguing at all, even if this is irrational or damaging to the project. There will be minimal conflict but also a lack of creativity and critical thinking; the main issue is that people will come to a conclusion before even evaluating their decision effectively.

After learning about what Groupthink entails, we will now look into ten ways through which you can beat the herd. Some tips from the experts include:

1. Plan for Everything

If a risky plan is being discussed, it is advisable to come up with plans for all conceivable scenarios. It does not mean that the group will fail; however, it is good to start by tackling the underlying problem as it is, rather than ignoring it.

2. Encouraging a Debate

When you get your way through a debate, you will feel good; however, the feeling will be short-lived, and the end result may also not be desirable. As a leader within a team, you should be bold enough to face the team members and emphasize how different ideas should be discussed further. People can also express their opinions while also challenging the opinions put across by others. For instance, in business, happy-talk may be common; however, there should be another discussion that will ensure that people get to learn more about different business endeavors. The main focus here is on increasing your knowledge base. By doing so, you will be able to overcome Groupthink.

3. Looking for Different Personalities

In a group, the majority of the members should possess different personalities. Some of these personalities include the presence of a creative problem solver, an unorthodox thinker, a person who works well under pressure, and the person who judges the opinions that have been put across by other members of the group. The judgment should be made in an objective manner. Make sure that you have looked for people who have varying styles of communicating and thinking.

4. Acknowledge the Bias in the Data

Some leaders may assume that by relying on data, they may eliminate Groupthink. At times, an analyst may not issue accurate information, and they may pick different pieces of information in a bid to please the managers. Based on this inaccurate information, the managers may be reassured about the decisions that they have implemented, and they may fail to make improvements. After some of the misleading insights are approved, they may be harder to challenge. As a leader, you should make sure that you have not revealed your "hopes and dreams" to a data scientist that you have hired to mine and collect some information, as this might influence the report.

5. Reaching Out

Always invite people from other departments, especially if they have been affected by some of the decisions that you have made. Even if the invited people fail to attend the meeting, make an effort to reach out to other people within the company, and they should issue some feedback. People within an organization should avoid being influenced by the ideas within the group, and they may be willing to offer independent ideas and options.

6. Understand that Speed Can Kill

At times, when people reach a decision quickly, the group may be relieved. Speed can indeed kill, and that is why a group should not make a decision hastily. First, everyone should issue their own opinion. If a leader believes that the debate was not enough, they should delay the decision and make sure that the other group members have carried out further research.

7. Increasing Awareness

As a leader, you should focus on ensuring that you have created awareness within the group in a bid to prevent Groupthink. The leader should ensure that people are aware of what Groupthink is and how it takes place. Also, they should be informed about the consequences of Groupthink.

8. Take Part in Open Discussions

While in a group, it is advisable to create a culture whereby the employees will be encouraged to analyze the situations accordingly while issuing feedback and sharing information.

9. You Should Not Shoot the Messenger

When engaging in an open discussion, you should avoid a lot of criticism. At times, when a person comes up with an alternative opinion, they may be criticized by the other members. People within a group should learn more about critical listening skills.

10. Assign the "Devil's Advocate"

As a leader, you should consult one or two members and ask them whether they would be comfortable playing the role of the devil's advocate. The group should be divided twice, and one team should look into the pros, whereas the other team should focus on the cons of a certain opinion.

We have looked into ten ways through which Groupthink can be eliminated. There are also other ways through which Groupthink can be eliminated, and they include:

- **Consulting Some of the Subject Matter Experts**

When discussing a very important topic, some subject matters may be involved, and they may be present in the group. In some instances, the group may have to hire a subject expert externally. A subject expert is a person who understands everything about a certain subject, and they can offer some insight into the present consequences associated with a specific opinion. Also, they can look into some of the present alternatives that will be suitable in each case.

- **The Decisions Should Be Documented**

After the group has reached a decision, the members can go ahead and document the information.

- Some of the possible solutions and each option should be analyzed thoroughly.
- The present situation and some of the associated issues.
- The recommended solution and why it is preferable.
- A plan that is implementable. The budget and the timeline should also be presented.

- **A Group May Ask for an Opinion from Another Team**

At times, some of the group members may not be comfortable with the decisions that they have made, and they may solicit some opinions from another team. The other team will review the provided document, and give feedback.

Finally, it is good to note that when collaborating as group members at the workplace, the learners should sit back as a way of avoiding Groupthink and the presence of ideas that lack a touch of creativity. If one of the leaders can make good use of the creativity demonstrated by one of the group members, they can channel it accordingly, and they may produce a more desirable outcome.

Chapter 14: Body Language: Speed-Reading and Sending out the Right Message

Perhaps you have been wondering how life would be if someone could read another person's mind. Some people know how to make good use of their intuition for such issues. But others are not exactly good at it. For people who cannot use their perception, there is one ideal option left. It is learning how to study a person's body language. That said, it is a fact that people can get up to 45 percent of information from nonverbal communication. Experts specializing in body language have written in the past that people can often study the gestures as well as other additional body movements of an individual to unmask the character of a person and then tell what they think or, better yet, feel. Mimics can also be used to analyze a person's character. Other professionals have added that you should pay attention to various signals sent by other people without them realizing it. While most people may not consider narcissism as well as psychopathy desirable traits in friends as well as lovers, most of us are strangely drawn toward people with the mentioned personality traits. As such, "mean girls" are usually popularly known in school.

Vampires are known to be sex symbols. But in recent research, it was concluded that people commonly referred to as individuals with dark personalities are physically attractive compared to others. So, what is it really about these dark personalities that make these individuals as appealing as stated in the research studies? What makes them tick? Why do people fall into their trap? The answers to these questions can assist us in comprehending what makes individuals with such personalities successful when it comes to exploiting other people.

To test that, two professionals are known as Nicholas Holtzman, as well as Michael Strube of the prestigious Washington University, studied the relationship between people's tendencies and their attractive nature. They also analyzed the relationship between people and psychopathy, in addition to Machiavellianism. These researchers wanted to determine whether the traits mentioned, which are also referred to as the Dark Triad, are directly linked with the ability to enhance a person's physical appearance. To test the idea, these professionals decided to invite up to 100 students into a laboratory. Every student was asked to take a photograph immediately. After that, every student was asked to put on a grey pair of pants and a shirt. The women in the team were asked to cleanse their faces by removing makeup. Individuals with long hair were asked to wear their hair into a ponytail. The students were photographed.

The two professionals took the two sets of photographs and compared them. This was in terms of their physical appearance. They were in a position to determine their looks, including how attractive every student was. The professionals assessed these candidate's personalities, including their tendencies towards psychopathy. Candidates were asked to rate themselves and then share their friend's contact details. It was decided that their friends should leave ratings too. The combination of peer ratings was then used in calculating the set of various personality scores for students. The ratings provided by students based on narcissism and psychopathy were also merged to create a major composite known as the Dark Triad.

The Dark Triad was pretty much correlated with the attractive candidates. But, the score of the Dark Triad was not primarily related to the physical attractiveness of the candidates once they were stripped down to basic clothes and hair. People who had a dark personality trait were not seen as physically attractive compared to others, especially when you take away their freedom when it comes to wearing their clothes as well as makeup. People who had dark personalities were good at dressing up. Following a detailed introduction, it was concluded that every student should fill out a survey that asked their opinion regarding first impressions. The candidates who scored high marks when it comes to narcissism were likable. These findings have reinforced initial research indicating narcissists are more well known and liked than others, at least at first.

Candidates seen as likable were more narcissistic with flashier appearances and confident body language. Researchers concluded that narcissists are good at carrying as well as presenting themselves in such a way that they can easily impress others instantly. This is also an additional reason why it is crucial to take time to judge a person's character when meeting for the first time. The first step of resisting a person with a Dark Triad trait is not easy. If they are physically attractive,s this is also automatically attached to other positive traits, in the "halo effect." When someone is perceived as physically attractive, we may assume that they are kind in nature as well as more confident. To create an advantageous environment, the person needs to look attractive physically. When a person's physical attractiveness merges with their confidence they are more effective when it comes to deceiving someone. It also appears that individuals with exploitive personalities are relatively more successful at this.

Analyzing Different Body Language

You may feel that you comprehend all the manipulation tactics, including how to use them to, win the hearts of your peers or family. However, it is still important to garner more information regarding body language and how you can persuade various people around you. While there are several differences in people, there are also a couple of similarities. To better analyze people around you, you need to find a few elements that can help you to connect with them by bringing you together rather than tearing you apart. It is also important to note that manipulation is a negative trait. We, therefore, emphasize the need to understand how to read body language. In this chapter, we shall look at some of the main body language cues involved in the Dark Triad and teach you how to analyze them:

Closing the Eyes

If the person you are talking with closes their eyes, then they are on the verge of telling a lie. You need to remember that it does not imply they are scared of you. Rather, it means that they are evasive because they do not want to deal with the situation at hand. They could also be trying to avoid you.

Presenting the Face

This is a gesture used to attract individuals of the opposite sex. When a person places their chin on the hands, they present their face to be viewed as if trying to say "This is me." Therefore, you are often allowed to enjoy what you are seeing. For men, it is important to memorize this kind of gesture to be in a position to catch a complimentary moment.

Arms on The Chest

The next body language we shall look into is the arms crossed over a person's chest. This is an ideal example of defensive individuals. It is often used to demonstrate that a person disagrees with certain opinions as well as the actions of others regardless of their relationship.

Touching the Nose

When an individual touches their nose when talking, it can always signify a couple of things. First, it could be rejection. Then secondly, it could be a way of demonstrating a person's dishonesty when it comes to what they are saying.

Palms Open

When a person opens their palms facing upward, it could be a symbol of being honest or open to a stated idea. That said, in older centuries, when individuals carried their weapons, the sign was used to indicate that they were armless and sincere. Over the years, it became a consistent practice indicative of innocence. When a person puts head in hands, it is an ideal example of a body language that could imply the individual is upset. Therefore, they may not be interested in showing their face. Locked ankles indicate that a person is nervous.

Rubbing the Chin

The chin is often rubbed when someone is trying to make a crucial yet viable decision. The person could be looking down or sideways. But they hardly know exactly what they want since they are thinking critically and deeply. The throat below the chin is also vulnerable, therefore, a predator can easily use it to attack an individual. Holding the chin is a protective measure for the throat. It is also one of the ways through which people act defensively. Holding the chin is also a symbol of being submissive.

Sending Out the Right Message

Without a doubt, it is vital to learn how to communicate nonverbally. This is usually in the form of someone's body language. The method has a significant impact on how the message is communicated and then received by other people. Nonverbal communication is also vital in business. Workplace communication drives various activities between customers and service providers.

Give these tips a try:

Watch Out for Yourself and Others

When in the process of communicating with other people, you should be attentive to the type of messages you intend to send via your body. Do your words match the nonverbal language? In case they do not, then it is time to fix them. That said, people are often gifted with the knowledge to grasp the nonverbal cues.

Remember to Maintain Eye Contact

It is crucial to maintain eye contact, especially when talking with other people, such as coworkers and employers. With eye contact, you shall be building trust. At the same time, you will be able to use eye contact to send a relatively strong message to other people if you are not comfortable.

Chapter 15: Creating your OWN Thoughts

We are often told to guard our thoughts since they tend to influence our actions, and that our thoughts have power.

But we rarely look at the origins of our thoughts, since we may not necessarily like what we find; some of us may discover that our thoughts are influenced unconsciously by trauma, fear, lack of knowledge on a particular subject, or maybe we have even been influenced or manipulated by a friend or partner.

How many times have you seen an Instagram post showcasing the latest fashions and thought to yourself, "I must have that" Or when you were enjoying some screen-time and a marketing ad for a new product, you immediately thought "I must have that too."

What of Groupthink? I guarantee most of us may have fallen victim to this one and have been part of a group. Not all outside influence is bad; as a matter of fact, some can be very instrumental in ensuring we come to the right conclusions. However, at times when engaging in Groupthink we may feel too afraid to voice our individual thoughts that differ from the group. There are various options or alternatives to discuss but this chapter will focus on one solution without serious deliberations.

So how does one go about the process of creating their own thoughts without any influences? Well here are some tips to create your own thoughts:

1. Creating Your Own Identity

This involves creating one's own sense of self. That means clearly defining your interests and preferences. Having a clear picture of who exactly you are, what you love to wear, and how you would love to look. This will help you not to fall victim to influence from media ads that tell you what you should wear, what products you should use, or how you should look.

2. Acquiring Adequate Knowledge

One should aim at having adequate knowledge about a subject or situation before forming an opinion. You should learn to constantly obtain knowledge either from reading books, observing situations, and listening keenly before coming to a conclusion.

For example, this can help so you aren't influenced to purchase a product or service which you may not be fully aware of.

3. Learning to Be Flexible

You should not imagine that only specific solutions will work for specific problems, sometimes they might. But if they don't, always be open to discover other solutions to the problem, weigh in on their pros and cons and try to see if they could work. And before you say "no," also aim to look at each solution from all different perspectives, then see if they have any negative consequences and if they harm anyone. If they don't, then try to implement them or factor them in as possible solutions.

4. Learning to Point out Possible Biases

We can often find it hard to judge a situation for what it is, as we often unconsciously factor in our cultural biases or our own upbringing and other people's opinion. Therefore, we end up deciding from a wrong perspective. Try to take the time to evaluate the situation without any biases, observe things first-hand, and then form very clear opinions about the subject or situation.

5. Not Caving in to Fear, Pressure and Guilt

Sometimes we may find it hard to voice our opinions if they differ from the group's, as we may fear that it will cause disagreements or for us to have labels. However, it is important to stand by your opinions regardless, since sometimes it may be the right thing to do. Other times it may just be the brilliant idea that everyone has been waiting to hear, furthermore, in a healthy argument, it is important to have everyone's opinion before you come to any conclusions.

Benefits of Creating Your Own Thoughts

While you may be enjoying your newfound power to create your own thoughts and opinions without any hindrances, here are some of the other benefits you may receive:

1. You tend to become more interesting to others since every time they have conversations with you, you challenge their opinions and thoughts.

2. You are constantly self-improving since you are always trying to seek different perspectives toward different situations. And you are always looking for different alternative situations to different problems.

3. You become more alert toward any persuasion or influence from the media.

4. You tend to gain respect from the people around you as they value your opinions since they are always original. They also value the fact that you are constantly standing up for them.

5. Your mind and mind power are always developing.

6. You develop trust in yourself and your abilities and therefore end up having great self-confidence.

Tips to Identify That You May Not Be Creating Your Own Thoughts

While creating your own thoughts can be quite essential and beneficial, sometimes, you may find yourself taking a few steps back. When you do, here are some of the tips that can let you know that you aren't thinking for yourself:

1. You may not take the time to evaluate things or situations before forming opinions on them.

2. You may find yourself doing some things the same way since they have always been done that way.

3. You may slowly find yourself buying into stereotypes based on sex, race, or culture.

4. You may find yourself being easily swayed by the media, another person, or a group of people.

Creating your own thoughts is very important as you get to form very clear opinions that help you in making very insightful decisions.

Conclusion

I hope you enjoyed reading *Dark Psychology: Master Persuasion, Negotiation and NLP and Unlock the Power of Understanding Manipulation, Deception, Mind Control, Human Behavior, Psychological Warfare, and Brainwashing.* I also hope that this Dark Psychology handbook was informative when it comes to learning more about Neuro-Linguistic Programming (NLP), master persuasion, and psychology, with regard to how people are manipulated and how to avoid manipulation.

The book has also been published with the sole aim of impacting people's lives positively. Always remember that you should focus on the chapters that discuss more about the strategies used by manipulative people and how you can avoid becoming a victim. After all, no one likes being manipulated by another person. I bet that you do not want to be associated with manipulative people, and some of the strategies that have been highlighted in this book will ensure that you can navigate your way out of some tricky situations.

Sources

https://www.darkpsychology.co/dark-psychology/
https://www.youtube.com/watch?v=UAIEvoz_RJA
https://www.psychologytoday.com/intl/blog/toxic-relationships/201812/how-spot-narcissist
https://psychcentral.com/lib/how-to-recognize-a-psychopath/
https://www.spring.org.uk/2018/08/machiavellian-personality-disorder.php
https://www.psychologytoday.com/intl/blog/sex-murder-and-the-meaning-life/201412/the-four-dark-personality-traits
https://www.youtube.com/watch?v=juhqwEf8kSY
https://www.apa.org/monitor/2014/02/criminal-mind
https://online.maryville.edu/online-bachelors-degrees/forensic-psychology/historys-famous-crooks/
https://www.darkpsychology.co/cybercriminal-minds/https://www.effective-living.com/3290/warning-signs-of-a-criminal-mind/
https://openpsychometrics.org/tests/SD3/
https://www.youtube.com/watch?v=sUCG3osf4lA
https://www.youtube.com/watch?v=qL33TRP7qiE
https://www.cracked.com/article_19646_5-creepy-forms-mind-control-youre-exposed-to-daily.html
https://interestingengineering.com/the-cias-mind-control-and-lsd-program-mk-ultra
https://www.psychologytoday.com/us/basics/deception
https://www.fraud-magazine.com/article.aspx?id=4294971184
https://www.youtube.com/watch?v=P_6vDLq64gE&t=63s ,
https://www.inc.com/justin-bariso/an-fbi-agent-s-8-ways-to-spot-a-liar.html
 https://www.thehealthy.com/family/relationships/how-to-spot-a-liar/
https://www.theguardian.com/commentisfree/belief/2009/may/27/cults-definition-religion

http://cultresearch.org/help/characteristics-associated-with-cults/
https://psychcentral.com/blog/media-manipulation-of-the-masses-how-the-media-psychologically-manipulates/
https://exploringyourmind.com/10-strategies-of-media-manipulation/
https://newseumed.org/cantdupeme
https://www.wvik.org/post/why-political-propaganda-works-and-how-spot-it
https://www.historians.org/about-aha-and-membership/aha-history-and-archives/gi-roundtable-series/pamphlets/em-2-what-is-propaganda-(1944)/what-are-the-tools-of-propaganda
https://spectrum.ieee.org/computing/software/how-political-campaigns-weaponize-social-media-bots
https://study.com/academy/lesson/what-is-psychological-warfare-definition-techniques-examples.html
https://medium.com/@womanistpsych/psychological-warfare-tactics-manipulating-your-vote-182d754961cd
https://www.listeningpartnership.com/insight/master-manipulator/
https://inlpcenter.org/what-is-neuro-linguistic-programming-nlp/
https://www.the-secret-of-mindpower-and-nlp.com/NLP-techniques-for-persuasion.html
https://happyrubin.com/nlp/negotiation/
https://theplaidzebra.com/the-6-nlp-techniques-that-will-turn-you-into-an-expert-negotiator/
https://www.verywellmind.com/what-is-groupthink-2795213
https://highfive.com/blog/8-steps-to-avoid-groupthink
https://www.youtube.com/watch?v=4jwUXV4QaTw
https://www.insider.com/subtle-signs-that-youre-talking-to-a-psychopath-2018-2
https://www.businessinsider.com/how-to-tell-if-you-are-talking-to-a-psychopath-or-narcissist-2017-12#psychopaths-tend-to-use-emotional-language-without-displaying-much-feeling-3
https://www.huffingtonpost.co.uk/dr-raj-persaud/dont-walk-this-way-how-yo_b_6509478.html

https://www.inc.com/amy-morin/advice-from-a-therapist-5-ways-to-with-a-psychopath-at-work.html

https://www.iflscience.com/brain/manipulative-psychopaths-lose-their-mischievous-powers-when-talking-online/

https://www.essentiallifeskills.net/think-for-yourself.html

https://www.aconsciousrethink.com/8349/thinking-for-yourself/

Section 2: NLP

The Ultimate Guide to Using Neuro-Linguistic Programming for Persuasion, Negotiation, Mind Control, and Manipulation, along with Dark Psychology Techniques to Increase Your Social Influence

Introduction

This book provides the Ultimate Guide to using neuro-linguistic programming for persuasion, negotiation, mind control, and manipulation along with Dark Psychology Techniques to increase your social influence.

It focuses on the practical NLP methods and techniques for persuasion, negotiation, mind control, and manipulation, along with tips to help you understand and avoid dark psychology tactics. It provides simple, straightforward NLP techniques for self-development and enhancing your skills in dealing with the people around you, as well as aids for creating a positive, meaningful environment.

The book then draws you toward Dark NLP psychology and its tactics. You may study these tactics and decide for yourself as to how you can use them in your daily life to gain a positive advantage from them.

The book is divided into three parts:

Part 1- The Essential of NLP

Part 2- The NLP Practicum

Part 3 – The Dark Side of NLP

Each part is comprised of its own uniquely structured content and describes the wide variety and range of techniques to be used in specific situations and for varied purposes. The techniques can be used to better business skills, improve interpersonal skills, and discovering the formula to live your life your way while striking a balance with the ethics, morals, and principles that you have set for yourself.

NLP is an effective behavioral program for personal transformation and business-related purposes. Training in NLP is meant to improve current behavior as well as skill levels in management and leadership, coaching and mentoring, and marketing and sales, enhancing your charisma at a personal and professional level and helping you to excel in building rapport and persuasiveness.

Although NLP techniques have not been scientifically proven, they have been shown over the years to help its users:

- Get a grip on their life
- Communicate their message more precisely by training in the use of language and communication
- Target outcomes and goals that have the most impact
- Formulate strategies on how to achieve target and goals
- Gain the confidence to lead a business
- Enhance and develop business results
- Find what drives them, decide what they value the most, and focus on how to achieve it
- Provide a sense of direction in life
- Formulate the rules to success
- Understand failure and utilize lessons learned to refine criteria and attempt achievements again
- Find ways to lead a happy and meaningful life

- Identify and find solutions for conflicts at a personal and professional level
- Overcome hindrances in personal and professional relationships
- Find ways to gain the courage to pursue dreams
- Set higher targets and gain as much as they rightfully deserve
- Offer professional development-training programs
- Elevate their principles and beliefs
- Build rapport at a personal and professional level
- Develop public speaking and presentation abilities
- Find ways to change morally unacceptable behavior
- Grow and develop businesses
- Excel in coaching and mentoring
- Formulate coaching programs as a business leader
- Persuade a team to work for a socially beneficial cause

The latter part of the book focuses on the use of manipulation for positive personal benefits and gaining a fair advantage. It elaborates on using NLP tools and techniques to manipulate a mass of followers, to create social impact, or develop into an effective leader. It describes using NLP for attraction, weighing the pros and cons of Dark NLP to make sure that the tools and techniques do not control your mind.

Part 1: NLP Essentials

Chapter One: What is Neuro-Linguistic Programming?

This chapter is a theoretical introduction to Neuro-Linguistic Programming. It gives you an overview of how it was founded, its underlying principles, key benefits, and theoretical modeling systems, metaprograms, and examples you may find useful.

"Neuro" refers to the neurological network – the environment that is perceived by the senses, and the sensory knowledge that is consciously and unconsciously converted into our thinking processes. In turn, these thoughts can influence our physiology, emotions, and behavior.

"Linguistic" refers to how language is utilized to make sense of the world. Language plays an important part in understanding and perceiving the world.

"Programming" refers to the learning process – the various internal methods and built-in models we use to learn things and make decisions.

How NLP Was Founded

Neuro-Linguistic Programming (NLP) was created in the 1970s by founders R. Bandler and J. Grinder of the United States and is a semi-scientific approach to interaction, self-development, and counseling. The founders stated that neurological processes (neuro), language (linguistic), and behavioral patterns that have been learned from experience (programming) are interconnected and can be adapted to specific purposes in life. Bandler and Grinder suggested that NLP techniques can "design" the capacities of people so that everyone can improve their abilities.

NLP can deal with psychological issues like phobias, anxiety, tic disorders, mental illness, vision problems, asthma, common cold, and learning disabilities. It is also used to treat emotional and behavioral problems. NLP opponents argue the concept is not scientifically proven and is not even regarded as entirely scientific. Science-based reviews assert that NLP has been founded on inaccurate analogies of the mechanisms of the mind that are incongruent with existing cognitive theory, and therefore encompasses many factual inaccuracies.

Reviews have maintained that studies on NLP work presented major critical flaws, and have struggled to prove Bandler's, Grinder's, and other researchers' "extraordinary assertions" to be faulty. Nevertheless, NLP has already been embraced as a tool of management training by authorities, counselors, and mentors in companies that conduct seminars.

The Early Development of NLP

NLP involves a method called modeling and a collection of approaches developed by Bandler and Grinder. Some were learned from the research of M. Erickson, V. Satir, and F. Perls. The concepts of G. Bateson, A. Korzybski, N. Chomsky (especially transformative grammar), and Carlos Castaneda were also investigated by Bandler and Grinder.

The founders believed that their approach would convert the structure and complicated human activity that is evident in the treatments carried out by Perls, Erickson, and Satir, as well as other therapists; the codified elements derived from the structure could then be learned by others. The therapists compiled a book in 1975 named "The Structure of Magic: The Language and Therapy Book" that attempted to codify the therapeutic methodologies of both Satir and Perls.

The founders claimed that they had employed their own modeling system to create the Meta-Model, the framework to collect data and address questions about the language and cognitive patterns of the consumer. They asserted that their transformative grammatical principles provided a more accurate description of the fundamental structure and challenges of linguistic distortions, defining generalizations and restoring information that was erased in the individual's statements. Anchoring, possible pacing, and representation structures were also drawn from Satir.

Bandler and Grinder described the Milton Framework— a version of Milton Erickson's allegedly hypnotic language— as artsy and metaphorical. Merged with the Meta model, the Milton model is utilized to trigger a half-conscious state of mind receptive to implied psychological recommendations. Other than Satir, neither Bandler nor Grinder worked with the writers or researchers they describe as sources. Chomsky has no connection at all with NLP; his initial work was meant to be a hypothesis rather than a treatment.

André M. Weitzenhoffer, an expert in hypnosis, points out that "the serious drawback of the linguistic analysis made by the founders is that it is concluded on assumptions that aren't really tested and backed with relevant data." Stollznow also pronounced NLP to be less than credible.

More recently, Bandler claims to have utilized linguistics and holographic patterns to design NLP. The models that form NLP are structured models formulated from numeric, rational principles, including scientific formulas and the theoretical constructs underpinning holography. The drawback here is that McCledon, Spitzer, and Grinder don't talk about mathematics or holography in accounting for the NLP construction.

The founder recalls their thoughts at the time of formulating the code, from 1973 to 1978, when they focused mostly on planning a campaign guided by Thomas Kuhn's work on the structure of scientific revolution to overthrow the existing paradigm. He perceived it as an advantage that none of the founders were trained psychologists or learned in that sector and thought that useful when designing a therapeutic application. This was also an important aspect that Kuhn noted when he studied the transformation of the paradigm.

A few scholars like Robert T. Carroll were contradicting the founder's efforts and condemning the fact that he formulated NLP without a proper understanding of Kuhn's concepts. According to Carroll, the shift in paradigm wasn't pre-planned but was a result of the effort made scientifically regarding the paradigm that generates information that is inefficacious within the existing paradigm, thus creating the shift from a necessity to adopt a new system.

While developing NLP, the founders were not paying attention to the design crisis relating to psychology, and they didn't get data that was caused by that phenomenon.

How NLP was Commercialized

The NLP system was promoted, and its techniques were accepted for use in the relevant industry and business sectors. The founders decided to depart from focusing on academia and instead propagate their materials through events and presentations focusing on individuals or groups who were keen on discovering changes.

At that period, the NLP movement was formed by a community of therapists as well as learners and gained worldwide attention. Many of the renowned self-help experts and life coaches of today have explored NLP and use it in their education. For instance, Grinder was trained by Tony Robbins.

Since then, the campaign has lost focus. Some opposing factions who do not buy into NLP say it has no scientific basis. However, the ideology is still being studied extensively and used in academic and non-academic arenas.

NLP- Its Underlying Principles

NLP is based on three main principles beneath which lie other components and concepts that relate to the main ones.

1. Subjectivity. You live your life very subjectively, and this leads you to create a subjective representation of all your encounters. The representations are created by your language and the five senses of the body. The subjective encounters we are consciously aware of are an accumulation of inputs from sight, hearing, touch, smell, and taste. An example is when you reminisce about a memory of a past event and while doing so you can see images, recall sounds, feel sensations, or smell odors from the event; also, you may think of something in a language that is a part of you. It is believed these types of experiences to have a perceptible structure and a sequence. NLP is described as the analysis of the subjective experience structure.

The actions pertaining to sensory representation can be understood. Behavior is widely perceived to include verbal communication as well as body language that is non-verbal, dysfunctional, non-adaptive, or compulsive.

Actions (in oneself and other people) can be altered by influencing these senses.

2. Consciousness. NLP relies on the concept that awareness transforms into conscious and non-conscious actions. Subjective representations that take place outside the consciousness of an individual comprise the "unconscious thought processes."

3. Learning. NLP employs an illustrative learning process — a term-modeling method— that systemizes and replicates the know-how of a model in any area. A description of the senses/language pattern of the relative experience of the subject during the implementation of expert knowledge is a significant part of the codification process.

NLP - Theoretical Model System

The Communication Model. The three key elements mentioned above form the fundamentals of the NLP theory and approach. The NLP communication model is a core concept of the program. This paragraph briefly addresses how NLP assumes social behavior takes place.

The NLP communication model fundamentally assumes that an individual is in a kind of constant behavioral loop. Your outside behavior always creates a reaction within you. In turn, the internal answers motivate an individual to react in a specific fashion or portray a particular external behavior. This external behavior creates another internal reaction, and the process continues like a cyclic response.

Also, your internal reaction to a particular external behavior is an effect of the internal state of mind and mental processes continually working inside your brain. The reaction is subject to the multiple ways in which you perceive the subjective experience. The internal cycle involves aspects like self-talk and what you are hearing in your mind, while the inner system is about feelings and emotions.

Techniques of NLP

The NLP idea is based primarily on the concept of a coping technique for each action and reaction in your internal and external behavior. To explain and modify human behavior, the program uses several concepts:

Modeling: Modeling was the grounds for the NLP concept. Modeling is believed to provide insight into the individual's belief system and the psychological anatomy of a person. It is used to understand the built-in mental techniques of the person, which affect all other aspects of thought and behavior.

Modeling mainly identifies the tactics or psychological patterns that a person uses to do things. The way an individual learns new information, or a new skill, can be an example of modeling.

You would have to model three things to learn to speak a language like Spanish. Initially, you would develop a vocabulary of the language. This is meant to enable you to understand, for example, that "*gato*" means "cat."

Then you would learn the syntax. Syntax indicates your ability to combine words properly to make a phrase or sentence. The ability to say, for example, "My name is Alexa."

In the third part of modeling, you would learn to employ mouth movements to speak and sound the way you should when speaking Spanish.

NLP contends that not only can you find these models in every aspect of your social behavior, but that you can alter your behavior by changing the patterns that precipitate your usual behavior. You can discover, for instance, the patterns used to respond to emails and remedy the problematic element of your model if you are not as efficient in replying to emails as you wish to be.

Strategies of NLP for Internal and External Interactions. In NLP Strategy Theory there is always posited a particular pattern of external and internal happenings that contribute to a certain result. You are probably going to witness a different outcome if you adjust the pattern and order.

Let's consider the example of how to want to improve your email. You are likely to most often use a specific set of patterns of both external and internal interactions to reply to emails. This could mean sticking to a particular time or a specific format, or varying your priorities based on to whom you are replying. This will not happen in the same manner if the sequence is disturbed or modified.

The five distinct senses are the key features of each approach: visual, auditive, kinesthetic, olfactory, and gustative. You might begin to compose an email, which would be your external behavior, but that action produces an inner experience of a specific image or taste which in turn causes you to behave in a particular way. Remember these five sensory sensations may occur both externally and internally.

When you meet an NLP specialist, they focus on recognizing your external and internal behavior. When you relate a story, they observe how your eyes rove, or your mouth moves, or your expression changes while you talk. These aspects help to identify your behavioral patterns and use them more productively to create a positive change.

The Test-Operate-Test-Exit Model (T.O.T.E. Model) of NLP

The T.O.T.E. concept was introduced by Bandler & Grinder. T.O.T.E. refers to a paradigm of various NLP techniques and is used primarily to demonstrate how an individual handles information. T.O.T.E. indicates Test, Operate, Test, and Exit.

Bandler and Grinder formulated the TO.T.E. theories, although they are somewhat derived from the book "*Plans and the Structure of Behavior*" by Miller, Galanter, and Pribam.

The T.O.T.E. model is primarily used to see which functions are responsible for your reactions, that is, to assess the set of particular strategies that function to determine your behavior.

In principle, the test examines the trigger that begins the strategy. As the mechanism continues to work, it will then again be checked to determine if the cycle is complete.

Take, for example, encouraging yourself to write emails. You would want to notice what factors drive you to begin writing in the first place. This is the "target trigger".

Operations are the next part of this model. The operating implication examines the external and internal methods required to continue the strategy.

You're going to carry out an alternative test at this point. In this part of T.O.T.E., you can compare if the initial test trigger and operation have induced a common strategy and conduct. If the test is successful and the same behavioral pattern is observed, the exit takes place. If not, this implies that the assumed trigger is not the correct one, or that the interactions have changed in the second stage of the operation.

Benefits of NLP

NLP has been widely used in various fields, and the system's proponents recognize that it can benefit most people from positive change in life. Some of the system's most common benefits are listed below.

Anxiety and Stress

A majority of therapeutic techniques, including NLP, prove efficacious in dealing with people facing anxiety Evidence and research shows that NLP contributes to alleviating the feeling of anxiety in individuals with claustrophobia during MRI scans.

NLP's linguistic system is primarily the vehicle for reducing anxiety and stress. An anxiety sufferer feels quite peaceful when they vent about their issues. Control workshops can offer people a rational understanding of the situation and improve the processes of adapting to stressful elements that disturb them.

Enhance Business Success

NLP can have an enormous effect on your work life, as it helps to transform your way of life in order to better meet your business objectives. It helps protect you from excessive hours of work and to find ways to engage in fruitful work with less time and effort. You're likely to be successful in business as you can channel positive behavior and eradicate unhealthy habits.

Develop Creativity

There is vast room for creativity in NLP techniques and strategies. You can begin to look at various concepts and techniques by considering the effects different sensory components have on your attitude. You can then observe common issues from a different perspective.

In addition, the plain fact that NLP relies on finding sequences to identify and improve your learning strategies is extremely relevant to commercial success. As NLP makes you understand how human behavior is taught, you find yourself in a position to leverage effective business tactics into your venture for success.

Eradicate Phobias and Fears

NLP works on discovering techniques that direct and enhance your behavior, so you can use them to overcome phobias or fears. Through NLP, the internal reaction you experience can shift when you come across something that causes you fear. You will learn strategies to regulate your feelings and remain calm and confident when you need to face the audience on stage or present during a meeting if you are someone who lacks confidence in public spaces.

Create Good Health and Relationships

Research suggests that the NLP has a very limited impact on healthy well-being; however, many believe that when anxiety is diminished and shifted after NLP approaches have been applied, people are better able to substitute good habits for the old bad habits. Since you are safe not having to think about an adverse health impact using NLP, it is easy to test if the system works for you.

Eventually, you will strengthen your interactions with others because the principles significantly improve insight into various human behaviors. You can better react to them and understand their negative approaches to life by understanding the way individuals work.

Chapter Two: Reframing to Change Your Mind

Having gained an insight into NLP, you must be curious to learn how to apply NLP techniques to improve your communication within yourself. Here's a warm surprise awaiting you. You already know the process of NLP and have utilized it on numerous occasions, which means it's not a skill you need to spend time learning! The only reason you are not aware of it is that it usually happens in your unconscious mind.

Although reframing is an unconscious process, it doesn't mean that everyone is capable of achieving the best possible outcome it has to offer. Have you ever fought a battle with yourself to break a bad habit and still not succeeded? Here's your answer. You can use reframing your mind, which is a core factor in NLP, and ensure that you emerge victorious this time.

Reframing in NLP

Choose a wall hanging in your home and imagine replacing its outer frame with a different one. Step back and take a look. Does it look the same to you? Most often, the answer will be "No." You have just used "reframing" to construct a new image from an existing one.

In NLP, "reframe" refers to the process of altering the meaning of a situation or communication by changing the frame surrounding it – where the frame could be the context, content, setting, and/or personal perception of the particular situation. Simply put, reframe means to look at a situation from a different perspective.

Reframing - A core presumption of the NLP approach is that every behavior is a function of a positive intention, regardless of it being favorable or non-favorable behavior. Reframing involves the process of separating a negative behavior from its positive intentions and holding the originator of the negative behavior as responsible for replacing the unfavorable response with improved behavior in accordance with the same positive intentions.

Now, if all that seemed too technical, here's a much simpler explanation.

Have you ever had an instance in life when you have been told off by your boss at work? You probably felt hurt and angry for being sidelined and might have been tempted to send in your resignation. Another way of interpreting the whole situation would be to accept the constructive criticism and use the opportunity to improve your efficiency.

The positive intention of this behavior is to move forward in life and past the point of being sidelined by your boss. The negative behavior is to get angry and be hurt and send in your resignation. The more positive behavior is to accept criticism and improve oneself. The positive behavior and negative behavior are two possible reframes for the situation with the boss. The process of choosing a positive outcome over the negative consequence when assessing the situation – that is reframing!

Do you now understand how reframing is a part of everyday life? We use it repeatedly to interpret all that happens around us. Whenever we try to draw meaning from events in our lives, we are choosing one perspective over numerous possibilities – which ends up defining our lives and decisions. Knowing the process of reframing helps to limit collateral damage to oneself by choosing a better alternative path of interpretation.

Types of Reframing – Content and Context

Content Reframe – Have you ever been in the situation where you were disturbed due to a power failure during a presentation, but your colleague managed to remain calm and continued talking smoothly under the same conditions? The meaning you have attached to the situation (that your presentation is doomed due to power failure) is different from that of your colleague. What you choose to focus on in an event determines the outcome of your behavior. The power failure in itself has no meaning attached to it other than it being an interruption of the power supply. If you choose to perceive the power failure as a disturbance, then you are likely to get annoyed. Contrastingly, if you choose to use power failure as an opportunity to recollect your thoughts, you are going to be geared up to resume the presentation when the power is back.

Therefore, content reframing is the process of looking for a different meaning in a situation.

Context Reframe - changing the situation to give the same behavior a different meaning. Behavior doesn't have the same meaning in all contexts. For example – a habit of using different colored ink to decorate your short notes when self-studying is useful for highlighting different topics, but not practical when you are writing an exam paper under timed conditions.

In context reframing the original behavior is left unchanged. You only relocate the behavior to a new place, a different situation, and thereby change the meaning of it. Can you imagine a situation where a negative behavior such as procrastination can have a positive effect? Apply it to overeating! Delaying your dessert after a meal will have a positive effect on you by preventing overeating.

Six Steps You Can Use to Master the Process of Reframing

Although the process of reframing happens unconsciously, it is worthwhile to be able to acknowledge the sequence of events that bring about this change in perception, mainly because it will help you engage in reframing consciously.

Reframing can be practiced in six stages. For the benefit of your understanding, the following stages have been illustrated with an example.

Step 1: Identification - recognize which negative feeling or behavior needs to be changed.

For instance – you always find yourself sitting up the entire night trying to complete your assignment the day before the deadline because you are procrastinating until the last day. The negative behavior you need to change here is delaying your work.

Step 2: Communication - identify the part of your unconscious which is causing this unfavorable behavior and try to initiate a conscious mode of communication between the two of you (let's call the unconscious mind "the mediator", for reference's sake). It would be helpful at this stage to pay close attention to any sensory signal (e.g., mental image, sound, tactile effects) in response to your request. Remember to appreciate the responsiveness of the mediator, as it always helps to be on positive terms with each other.

Realize that it is your internal organizer which is inefficient in task management. Take a minute to tap in your organizer and ask if it's willing to change its course of action for the better. You might receive a response in the form of a mental acknowledgment or slight change in sensations, so we pay close attention!

Step 3: Positive Intent – isolate the positive intention of the mediator. By doing so, you can separate the negative behavior from the positive intent and try to alter the undesirable trait while preserving the intention. Identifying positive intent also serves a second purpose; it allows the mediator to have an optimistic view of itself, increasing self-efficacy, thereby being less resistant to change.

Realize that your intention here is to complete your task before the deadline so that you have sufficient time to review it. Even if your behavioral response was unfavorable in delaying your workload, it still shares the same positive intent as systematically completing your work. Acknowledging this will ensure that your path to change begins with an optimistic outlook and not due to shame or regret – which, trust me, is not going to make the rest of the steps any easier.

Step 4: Solutions - tap on the door of your creativity and devise improved alternative responses to satisfy the positive intent. Remember to appreciate once again the cooperation extended by your creativity.

Come up with possible alternatives to your approach towards task completion, such as,

• Use a target system where you break up the task into sub-components which you can achieve daily.

• Use a reinforcement schedule where you reward yourself with an incentive when you reach a target.

• Alert yourself using reminders on your mobile phone or pop-ups on your computer screen.

Step 5: Evaluation - present the alternatives to the mediator for evaluation. Negotiate and try to decide on a better behavior to replace the previous undesirable response. If the mediator is not satisfied with the options, then forcing it to accept a choice is not recommended as it will only yield a temporary relief and may have repercussions instead of internalization. Go back to step 4 and try to devise more acceptable alternatives.

Ask yourself if you are willing to try a different approach next time you are presented with an assignment. If your unconscious communicates that your alternatives are too unrealistic or require too much effort, develop more ideas that will make it comfortable. Do not guilt-trip your unconscious into conceding to your conscious demands.

Step 6: Objections and Internalization – if all has gone well and the mediator is satisfied with your alternatives, it will embrace your solutions and replace the negative behavior with a favorable output. However, a change in your behavior or perceptions might have consequences on another factor in the environment that might need to be addressed.

If you decide to stick to the target system, it might affect your time management skills. You will have to set aside time daily for the task, which means taking time off other commitments. This will require compromises and prioritization of your numerous other chores.

Finally, look for ways to internalize the new behavior so that you no longer require reframing for the same situation in the future.

When Do You Use Reframing?

Practically every day. You can use reframing when you feel frustrated, angry, hurt, out of sorts, sad, or any uncomfortable state of mind. If you are a healthy individual, you probably find it unpleasant to dwell on a negative state of mind for a long time and will look for a distraction to step out of your ruminating thoughts. Reframing will guarantee you the relief you seek. Ask yourself, "What else could this mean?" instead of "Why me?" and you will be able to shed some light on your predicament.

Is Reframing A Form of Denial?

A common misconception of reframing could be that you are overcoming a negative situation in life by sugarcoating it. In other words, are you denying reality by pacifying yourself with an artificial justification? Reframing is far from denial. Under content reframing, we concluded that an event has no specific meaning attached to it and will assume any connotation you give it. Therefore, reframing is a process of accepting reality and choosing to perceive it in a manner that is beneficial to oneself. When you experience a setback in life and decide to move on, it means that you have accepted the setback as a new opportunity in life to start anew instead of being a victim of life events. Reframing is a liberating way of thinking.

Useful Tips for Reframing

- Develop healthy self-talk – learn to appreciate yourself and your efforts and increase your use of positive vocabulary. Replace negative thoughts with positive ones.

- Ask yourself, "Is there another way of looking at this situation?"

- Challenge yourself to come up with three other explanations for the event. There is no better way of boosting your morale than by presenting it with a challenge to prove itself once again.

Self Help – think of possible reframes you could consider when reassessing the following situations

- You have planned an excursion with your friends, but it starts raining heavily on that day, and you have to abandon the idea
- An intimate relationship ends
- You get fired from your job
- You fail an examination

Chapter Three: Anchoring Techniques to Change your Life

Anchoring is yet another Neuro-Linguistic Programming technique that focuses on gaining control of and maintaining your emotional state. It is a simple process that has a profound effect on your well-being. And it's no surprise that anchoring, like all other NLP techniques, is a process that you engage in daily at an unconscious level.

This chapter will take you through the process of anchoring, providing an insight into how it originated, some common applications of anchoring, and a few useful tips to ensure the maintenance of your anchors.

What is Anchoring?

It is the process of forming an association between an external stimulus and an internal state whereby the internal state can be aroused by merely experiencing the external stimulus. The association refers to a neurological pathway that is established as a result of numerous pairings of the internal state with the external stimulus. The internal state could be either a positive or negative emotion. However, NLP uses only positive states to anchor, as the goal of anchoring is to make you feel good, and that can be achieved only if you associate positive feelings. The process might sound complex right now, but once you've read the entire chapter through, you'll realize that practically every action of yours is influenced by anchoring.

Let's use an example. Have you ever wondered why you wake up every morning from the sound of your alarm? It's because of anchoring! The sound of the alarm (which is the external stimulus) has been consistently paired with a state of wakefulness (internal state), which has resulted in the formation of an association between them so now the mere sound of the alarm will cause you to open your eyes.

Try changing the tone of your alarm and observe if it has the same effect on you. The majority of the time you will sleep through it and wake up late the following day because the sound of the new alarm has no built-in association with your state of wakefulness; therefore, it doesn't wake you up. But, give it a week or so and you will realize that you can to wake up as usual for the sound of the new alarm.

So, what did you learn from your experience with the new alarm? Repetition or consistency is an essential part of anchoring. The internal state has to be repeatedly paired with the external stimulus to establish the association called anchoring, but it is not the same for all types of anchoring. Certain associations can be built on just one instance of pairing. The necessity for repetition is dependent on the strength or frequency of occurrence of the stimuli.

How Did Anchoring Originate?

If you're curious to know a little bit of the history of anchoring, here it is. All credit goes to the Russian physiologist Ivan Pavlov who conducted a series of experiments with dogs. Pavlov observed an extraordinary response of the dog towards the food, which later was used to form the principle of classical conditioning. He realized that the dogs initially salivated at the presence of food, which was expected, as it is a natural response to salivate at the sight of food. However, as the series of experiments progressed, the dog began salivating at the mere sound of the footsteps of the researcher bringing the food, well before the food was presented to the dog. This phenomenon was termed classical conditioning, whereby a neutral stimulus (footsteps of the researcher) was paired with an unconditioned stimulus (food), that originally elicited an unconditioned response (salivating). Numerous such pairings resulted in the neutral stimulus becoming a conditioned stimulus (footsteps), which then elicited a conditioned response (salivating).

Anchoring is based on this principle of classical conditioning as it tries to form a stimulus-response association, which will produce the unconditioned response of feeling good whenever a person requires it.

Common Anchors in Your Daily Life

Imagine yourself driving. You approach an intersection, and the traffic lights turn red. You involuntarily step on the brake pedal and halt your drive – this is anchoring. Due to numerous occasions of stopping for a red light, you have formed an association between pressing the brakes and the red lights, which results in an unconscious effort to stop the car when you reach a red traffic light.

What about commercials that go on the television during your favorite program? As annoying as they may be, they serve the purpose of anchoring. Notice the content of these advertisements. They do not only include the picture of the product being promoted, right? They have so many extra stimuli involved, like children, pretty girls, good food, etc. Can you guess the reason for such inclusion? It's to tap on your pre-existing anchors, which make you feel good when you see yummy food, children, and pretty girls. By pairing their product with these stimuli, which provoke a sense of positive feeling within you, they aim to build an association between them: so that by the time you see the product of the store shelf, you involuntarily feel good and purchase it.

So next time you see a vehicle commercial full of pretty girls, pay close attention to what's happening within you.

Types of Anchors

In NLP Anchoring, the external stimulus acts as the anchor for your positive internal state. This external cue could take the form of any representational system which activates our sensory organs. The external stimulus can be any of the five senses:

- Auditory – a verbal phrase such as lyrics of a favorite song that makes you emotional
- Visual – an image of a holiday photograph which reminds you of all the good times
- Kinesthetic – a physical touch such as a hug from a friend which makes you nostalgic
- Gustatory – a specific dish which makes you feel sick in the stomach
- Olfactory – the smell of good perfume which makes you aroused

The Process of Anchoring

Although you are unconsciously aware of the process of anchoring, learning and practicing it consciously will give you the advantage of being able to control and maintain your emotional state and can prevent you from falling prey to pre-existing negative anchors in your life.

Imagine what it would be like be able to instantly shift from feeling angry and frustrated at being unfairly reprimanded to a state of peace and tranquility.

Here's how you can achieve it in just five steps:

1. Identify what you want to feel; for example, peaceful and calm.
2. Vividly recall an experience where you felt that emotion. Relive the situation and embrace the full force of the internal state, as if you

are experiencing it all over again. Think of an instance in life when you felt calm. Not just relaxed and cool, but truly at peace. It should be a state of high intensity of feeling, like maybe an episode of meditation. Now go back in time to that exact point in your life and relive it - literally. You can't be an observer of the event. You have to completely integrate yourself to hear, see, and smell all the stimuli in that environment. Only then will you be able to feel the same intensity of peace you experienced.

3. Anchoring - choose a specific external stimulus to act as your anchor. It could be kinesthetic such as touching your thumb and index finger together, making a fist, uttering a phrase aloud, etc.

Apply the anchor when you feel your peak state increasing and hold on until you feel the emotion begin to subside, then release the anchor.

When you find yourself reaching the peak of your state, and feel totally at peace, anchor your state by balling up your fist. Hold still until you feel the emotion beginning to fade. You have now formed a neurological association between the internal state of peace and an external cue of balling up your fist. Gently release the anchor by opening your palm

4. Change state - distract yourself by doing some other action such as looking out the window or reading something unrelated.

Change your mind by trying to recall the lyrics of your favorite song.

5. Test the anchor - now ball up your fist in the same manner as step 3 and observe if you can naturally drift back into that state of feeling. Don't resist, let anchoring just work its course.

Once again, ball up your fist and find yourself feeling the sensation of peace overtaking you.

If you don't find yourself being able to fire the anchor, go back to step 2 and repeat the process until you master it. Allow for sufficient time between setting the anchor (step 3) and firing it (step 5).

The Five Keys You Should Know About Successful Anchoring

You can easily remember the 5 keys using the acronym "ITURN".

1. The intensity of experience (I) - ensure that the experience you choose to anchor to is a situation of high intense emotion. (for example, when you want to anchor a confident state, do not choose a common experience such as driving. Although you may be highly confident of your driving skills, you are not in an intense mental state when you drive.)

2. Timing of the Anchor (T) - stay vigilant and apply the anchor when you are about to reach the peak of your emotional state. There is a minuscule time gap between applying the anchor and the acknowledgment on a neurological level. So, applying it just before you reach the peak will ensure that the anchor sets in at the peak state, which will provide optimum anchoring.

3. The uniqueness of the stimulus (U) - if it is a kinesthetic stimulus you seek, then choose a part of your body that is easily accessible while also being a part that is not commonly touched. Use an easily accessible point because you want to be able to call on the anchor immediately when required instead of reaching for a far corner of your physique. A rarely touched spot or gesture is used because you don't want to be unnecessarily firing the anchor every time that spot experiences contact or gesture is made, which might cause the anchor to lose its effectiveness after a while.

4. Replication of the stimulus (R) - reapply the stimulus many times to make sure that the anchor has been firmly set in your neurology (step 3 of the above procedure).

5. The number of times (N) - test the anchor repeatedly by firing, which will ensure that the new neurological pathway becomes a regularly used pathway that can be easily triggered when necessary.

Applications of NLP Anchoring

The prime use of Anchoring is to be able to manage your emotions and access resourceful states when you need them. To be able to replace negative and unwanted feelings with desirable ones is absolute freedom. There are many ways of using anchors to achieve this. Here are a few applications -

- State Management - this is the most basic use of anchoring. You call upon an internal state by touching your anchor when required. It's useful in situations like examinations, presentations, or interviews, where you might want to be highly confident.

- Stacking Anchors - to do this, you have to choose different situations that elicit the same or different emotions and stack them all at one point in your body. For example, you can create a stack of confidence anchors by forming multiple anchors of situations where you experienced peak confidence, or you can make a stack of peak positive anchors by anchoring different experiences of positive peak states.

This comes in handy when you want to experience multiple states such as a combination of happiness, confidence, and love. Your stack of anchors, when fired, will help you draw on all these states at the same time.

- Chaining Anchors - involves anchoring similar states on consecutive points of your body and firing them one after the other to experience a sequence of similar states. After a few trials of firing, you will realize that firing the first anchor is sufficient to activate the entire sequence of anchors. This is useful when you need to gradually transition from one state to another, building up your state until you reach the climax.

- Collapsing anchors - is a useful technique to remove a negative state and replace it with a positive one. It involves anchoring a negative state and a positive state at two separate points. Ensure that the positive state is more powerful than the negative state. Fire both states simultaneously, let both states overtake you, and then gradually release the negative state, followed by the positive state.

Is Anchoring Always Successful and Beneficial?

While anchoring is a technique you might count on to help you in tough situations, it might not always perform to your expectations. Like any other theory, anchoring isn't foolproof. It might cease to serve its purpose when the intensity of the negative emotion being experienced is greater than the power of the anchored state, or if the anchor hasn't been used often enough. During these moments you'll have to get creative and opt for a combination of techniques instead of stacking all the odds against one skill.

Just as a coin has two sides to it, anchoring also has its drawbacks. Not all anchors are beneficial. Can you think of a few harmful anchors? Here's a clue: How do you think phobias develop?

Chapter Four: Creating Rapport

In chapter 2 of this book, we looked at how a situation could take on a different meaning just by shifting the frame around it. In this chapter, we aim to give relationships a new meaning by adding a secret ingredient called rapport, which will improve the quality and efficiency of relationships. Rapport is no different from most NLP techniques in that it is an unconscious process that people indulge in. It is a natural occurrence in all intimate relationships.

Learning about the techniques of rapport will enable you to consciously apply them to relationships that lack depth and enhance the overall efficiency of communication. This chapter will discuss the value of building rapport, providing insight into how you can develop and maintain it in a relationship.

What is Rapport?

Have you ever met someone for the first time, and after a few minutes of interaction, felt like you've known that person all your life?

This is a direct result of rapport.

Rapport is an unconscious process of establishing a sense of trust and understanding with the other person. It is a form of communication characterized by complete responsiveness by both individuals in a relationship. it is, therefore, reciprocal. So, if you feel like you've known the other person your entire life after just interacting with him for 10 minutes, then he probably feels the same about you!

Rapport is created by a feeling of commonality between people. It is based on two fundamental principles -

- People associate with people who are similar to themselves (or their ideal selves).

- People reject those who are dissimilar to them or like those they don't want to be.

This suggests that people will be comfortable interacting with those with whom they share common ground or those to whom they can relate. At the same time, people tend to avoid those who seem different from them. This tendency of humans to choose who they interact with can be based on a primordial survival paradigm wherein people considered those within their clan as safe and those outside their territory as enemies.

Why Is It Important to Focus on Building Rapport?

Have you realized how comfortable you are with your best friend? It's because you have established rapport with them. Rapport puts people at ease and helps them open up to you. It results in the development of trust and understanding, which is critical to a mutually beneficial relationship. Building rapport will enable you to reach your target audience and convey your message effectively, which means that your efforts will bear fruit!

Imagine you are a clinical therapist, and your client walks in for a session. The individual starts talking in a very dull and monotonous tone to you, and it is evident that he/she is in a low mood. As a therapist, how will you try to lift the client's spirits?

Will you accuse the client of being ungrateful in life and admonish him/her to step out of the vicious cycle of depressive thoughts?

Or will you lower your tone to the level of the client's mood and try to strike up a conversation about how everyone is currently going through an equally tough time due to the economic crisis in the country?

The second alternative is the recommended course of action. You need to reflect on the mood of the client to help build rapport and put him at ease. This is known as mirroring. It will help the client see a friend within you, making him open up and be inclined to agree to your suggestions later on – known as Leading. The first alternative will simply alienate your client and discourage him from continuing therapy, which is why rapport is important. You need to be able to empathize and reach the person across the room instead of precipitating negative vibes which will distance them from you. Only then will you be able to deliver what they seek from you.

Who Is It Applicable To?

Have you ever tried to build that bond with your children to gain their trust and confidence, but failed miserably?

Have you ever wondered why some couples seem so in sync with each other that it's almost aggravating to you because you can't manage to get two words across to your partner efficiently?

Have you ever wondered why you are successful in selling a product to specific customers but fail with a majority?

Building Rapport might just be the solution to your worries. It is useful to everyone and anyone! After all, we humans are social creatures who are constantly in contact with people and building rapport with the people with whom we interact will ensure the optimum level of efficiency in communication.

Having stated that rapport is a style of communication, let's take a look at the different modes of communication and their actual contributions towards efficiency in human interaction. A common mistake is to overestimate the importance of verbal communication in an interaction. Statistics state that only 7% of human interaction is based on verbal communication. The remaining 93% of interaction is 38% tonality (the speed and volume of your tone) and 55% of non-verbal communication. Therefore, is it no surprise that a majority of rapport techniques focus on non-verbal communication styles.

Three Steps to Build Rapport

1. Matching and Mirroring

Matching is a process of physically replicating another person's actions. If the other person lifts his right hand, so do you. If he sits down on a chair, you sit too. If he crosses his right foot over the left, you do the same. It's very similar to the behavior of children and is rooted in observational learning, which states that children learn through modeling from their environment. Young children often repeat verbal phrases and copy actions of adults, which is a vital part of their learning process. This skill is retained in humans as we grow and manifests in the process of matching the behavior, words, and thoughts of those you with whom you identify.

You can try matching by choosing a random person and replicating his every move for a few minutes, making sure you are not in his direct line of sight, and your behavior doesn't draw attention to yourself (if this happens, it becomes mimicry and not matching). Match his posture, demeanor, and actions. At the end of a few minutes of duplicating his behavior, carry out an independent action (change your posture), and you will notice that he changes his posture too! This is evidence of matching taking place in real-time, at an unconscious level.

Mirroring – Go back to the example of the synchronized couple. Have you noticed how they move as a pair in unison as their every move compliments each other? This is known as mirroring. It involves physically reflecting another person's behavior on an unconscious level. You can try it by considering yourself to be a mirror for another person's actions. Start gradually by mirroring one aspect of their behavior. For example, if a person tilts his head to the right, you tilt your head towards the left. When you've managed it, you can include another action. For certain actions, you might have to wait for a time-lapse before mirroring the action. For instance, if a person gestures with his arm while talking, you wait for your turn to talk before gesturing with your arm.

By matching and mirroring behavior, you are creating a sense of similarity, which is a fundamental principle on which rapport is built. You might be under the impression that you are copying or mimicking a person by doing so, but actual matching and mirroring happen at an unconscious level. It takes place when both individuals carry out the same pattern of actions unaware that they are matching one another's behavior.

Behaviors and Actions to Match and Mirror

- The tone of voice – this includes the speed and volume of speech. If someone talks animatedly to you, increasing his pitch and tempo as he goes on, then you speak in the same vigorous tone and match his tone in your response, which will guarantee that you resonate well with the person, leading to rapport.

- Language - have you ever wondered why you babble when you talk to a baby, instead of speaking in a normal way? Well, it's because when you want to communicate effectively with someone, you need to talk in the same language as the other person, which is exactly what you're doing when you babble in baby language to an infant. Pay close attention to keywords or phrases used by the other person and repeat them in your response to them. So, the next time a client comes up and asks you "can you suggest a spectacular holiday destination?", you respond with "yes sir, this location seems like a "spectacular" holiday destination for you and your family, instead of saying "sure! I have a few wonderful holiday getaway plans lined up for you." *Do not interchange or paraphrase keywords* as it could have a different meaning to the other person.

- Body Language - match and mirror the other person's postures and gestures. If they tilt their head, you follow suit. If they gesture animatedly using their arms, you do the same, which will ensure they see themselves in you and pave the road to building rapport.

- Facial Expressions - try mirroring facial expressions, and you will find it easier to share the same emotions. If the person in narrating a tragedy and looking forlorn, then you remain downcast as well. It will help you empathize more efficiently.

- Eye contact - doesn't refer to maintaining eye contact for the whole duration of interaction! At the same time, don't look away when communicating. Eye contact is a primitive sign of making the person understand that they are being acknowledged. Therefore, maintain and break eye contact at a comfortable pace.

- Breathing - the single most profound factor that is easiest to replicate, and which will have instantaneous effective results! Try mirroring another's breathing rate, and you will find yourself falling into synchrony with the rest of the person's mental state.

- Touch and proximity - respond to a person's touch. A touch can sometimes communicate a million words and could be the magical factor required to establish rapport. If your child puts their arms around you in love, you circle your arms around them and return the hug. If your coworker pats you on your shoulder to acknowledge your efforts, you pat him back when you're leaving.

Proximity refers to personal space, which is crucial in a relationship. Pay attention and respect the need for space by the other individual. This will ensure that the person is at ease when communicating with you.

- Beliefs and values – try to assume the ideologies of the person you're communicating with, which will help in understanding where the person comes from and in offering non-judgmental solutions. This doesn't require you to internalize another's beliefs, it only serves the purpose of attaining rapport.

2. VAK Model of Information Processing

The VAK model proposes that people process information either visually, auditory, or kinesthetically, based on what they see, hear, or feel about the other person in a relationship. Paying close attention to how the other person processes information might be your gateway to win their confidence. For example, if you offer your hand to a stranger and he/she eyes you from crown to toe before responding, you know they sized you up visually before accepting you. For such a person, you need to look presentable and provide what they need to see in you (if it's a job interview - you need to show your confidence in taking up the role. If it's offering help to someone that has fallen in the street - you need to display kindness). But if you walk into an interview and the interviewee doesn't glance up from their papers, only acknowledges you with a sound, you know he's processing auditory information and so you speak what he wants to hear.

3. Pacing and Leading

Pacing is all about entering another person's world and becoming their model, but under their terms. It's almost similar to biofeedback, where you can match the other person's reality. It's a result of mastering the technique of matching and mirroring to the point where the person feels like they are in total synchrony with the other, and there is complete trust and understanding between them. It is the final step of building rapport, which will then facilitate the process of leading. You can check if you have skillfully paced another person by interrupting the synchronized pattern of behavior and observing if the other person unconsciously follows suit. Like taking a step backward when walking forward.

Leading is when you use the effect of pacing to influence or lead a person towards a particular goal: accomplishing rapport. In the example of the therapist and the client, the therapist will be able to lead the client to a healthier mental state once rapport has been established.

So next time you try to have a heart to heart conversation with your rebellious teenager or you're trying to convince a client to purchase your product, remember to apply the techniques of rapport, and you might find yourself successful in achieving your goal!

Part 2: NLP Practicum

Chapter Five: NLP Techniques to Persuade Anyone

Earlier, I outlined a detailed overview of NLP and how it could be used in terms of reframing your mind, utilizing anchoring techniques to create a diversion in the way you think, and creating a rapport through NLP techniques. This section is about persuasion and techniques of NLP that would be useful for you to persuade someone. The concept of persuasion is not scientific, but it is about understanding the human subconscious and the human mind. You take note of the other person's language and modify this language to change their behaviors.

This approach induces the individual to agree to a certain concept by allowing him to focus on the "HOW" of it rather than focusing on the "WHAT" of it. NLP is called Neuro-Linguistic Programming because it takes the words one speaks and reconstructs them to modify the way one thinks and behaves. This is sometimes perceived negatively, but a real NLP practitioner would only use his skills and talents to manipulate someone positively.

What is Persuasion?

Before I proceed further into NLP persuasion techniques, you must understand what persuasion is. Persuasion, also known as persuasiveness, is a form of creativity and requires mastery that can only be achieved by skillful and talented individuals. To persuade individuals and groups plays a significant role in becoming successful in your social and personal life.

Neuro-linguistic Programming practitioners and trainers have put forward exemplary approaches and techniques to persuade, which can be used in a variety of environments. Studies state that these techniques develop personal performances and help the individual maintain good intrapersonal and interpersonal relationships.

NLP methods of persuasion are selected by therapists during the treatment of individuals with mental difficulties such as phobias. To persuade someone entails a process of altering and rebuilding their opinions, beliefs, values, and behaviors towards an outcome. Humans are programmed in such a way that they find it extremely difficult to move out of their comfort zone no matter what their comfort zone is. For some individuals, even if their comfort is unhealthy, they wouldn't mind staying in it because, well, it's comfortable.

Persuasion is just not about forcing an individual to behave how we want them to behave; it is about allowing them to come out of their comfort zone to achieve a higher comfort zone after the discomfort of the change subsides. Simply put, an individual who regularly smokes will keep smoking because it is his comfort zone. To persuade or convince him will be a pretty challenging task because quitting is a discomfort for the person and during the non-smoking period this person might go through considerable discomfort, but afterward he is going to experience a higher comfort zone due to the absence of his unhealthy behavior.

For persuasion to be successful, the person trying to persuade the individual needs to figure out what is important to the individual. The persuader should identify factors that can eventually give the individual a higher level of comfort. For a person who finds staying at home and shunning social life comforting, the persuader should discover a factor that can allow them to move outside the box by helping them realize that although going out can be, once they achieve their goals, they are going to have a higher sense of comfort. This process needs a skilled persuader who will be able to assure the client that the behavior change is certainly going to make them feel more comfortable.

NLP Techniques for Persuasion

Moving on to the NLP techniques for persuasion, here's a couple of useful techniques that can help persuade someone.

1. Start a Conversation

Firstly, initiate your conversation on the correct path. This technique requires that the persuader make sure that the individual is familiar with the topic. Next is to be very clear and straightforward in what you say. Saying that "Anna failed" is a very unclear statement. Did you mean to indicate that Anna failed in her exams, an interview, or a quest? When you put forward a statement that can be misinterpreted, you need to make sure to use the correct vocabulary to explain it.

2. Pulsate the Person

The next thing is to know what pulsates the individual. Trying to get permission from your principal to organize a night party, you need to know what pulsates your principal. If your principal is someone who feels good when he is appreciated and praised, you can praise him as much as possible to get the permission. Give the individual a brief idea about the bigger picture in your words.

3. Build Rapport

Next is to build rapport while staying humble. If you are skilled enough to build rapport, then you are entitled to a pass to their trust.

A successful persuasion starts with a good rapport based on the trust the individual harbors towards the persuader.

4. Remain Calm, Composed and Humble

Staying humble, without seeming to be in competition with the individual and not making them feel that you think you are better than them, is critical during the persuasion process. Sending that sort of message will usually only cause the individual to stick strongly to his point, making it hard for you to persuade.

5. Absorb and Concentrate

Instead of figuring out what should be said next, absorb and concentrate on what is being said by the individual. Now, this is a pretty hard task; this develops gradually as you go along the way. When you pay enough attention to what the individual says, you will be able to reply to him properly, but if you were only thinking of what to say next, then you might go off topic, which can indicate your inattention and lead to a poor discussion. When the person is talking, make sure that you don't interrupt their statement just because you got the point; if that happens, the person might forget his point and get stressed about it.

6. Keep Track and Target a Suitable Time

One of the most important factors to consider when staring the persuasion process is time. If the person does not have enough time to have a discussion with you, then whatever you have to say might be not taken into consideration due to the lack of time they possess. Therefore, before initiating the conversation you need to be able to ask if the individual has enough time for a talk.

7. Be Respectful and Do Not Judge

Don't judge or disrespect anything that the individual says; you need to be able to empathize with what that individual says without giving him direct opposing comments or replies. You need to be well aware of the language that you use so that the other person does not get offended. Sometimes during the discussion, you might get emotional, which can lead to making the process like an argument, which indicates an unhealthy persuasion process.

Advantages of NLP

These NLP techniques can increase the level of influence that you exert on others. Companies that engage in marketing and sales completely depend on persuading their customers or clients to buy their products; the strategies presented in NLP guide these sellers and dealers to increase the chance of influencing their customers in making decisions. NLP also increases the personal performances of the person; NLP helps you to modify and replace your negative behaviors with more positive ones. These strategies also help you to improve your leadership style. Being humble and non-judgmental allows you to have a better style of communication, even outside the persuasion process.

Essentials for Persuasion

1. Empathy – this is an essential quality that a persuader requires. You should not only be thinking about yourself, but you also should try to put yourself in the other person's shoes and think about how they might be feeling. Empathy also helps deter you from being judgmental.

2. Listening Skills – only a good listener will be able to persuade another person; a person who is always ready for an argument will never be a good listener. If you want to be a good and positive persuader, you need to be able to listen to what the other individual says and pay attention to their body language as well.

3. Indirect and Clever Commands – people tend to be more responsive to suggestions than questions. For example, instead of using the words "Would you like to go to the concert?", you can say "Come, let's go to the concert"; this motivates a more positive response from the individual.

4. Restrict The Choices That You Provide – try not to allow the individual to say "No", or at least make it hard as possible for the individual to say "No." Taking the same example, instead of asking, "Will you be able to stay long at the concert?", ask them, "Would you like to stay here for three hours or four?". The latter question makes it hard for the individual to say a "No."

5. Allow the Person to Visualize – successful persuaders always help the client or the individual to visualize so that they can convince them. An example would be, "this concert will make us scream the lyrics of our favorite songs."

6. Always Make It Simple as Possible – trying to convince the other person by bragging will only be a failure; keep it as simple as possible and remember you should never put their views down.

Chapter Six: The NLP Negotiator: Effective Tactics

Life is full of negotiation, and at some point, you will have to negotiate for some reason or another. Think of all the activities that you do on a regular day and try to figure out if, in any of those activities, you could have gotten away with no negotiation. The simplest of things, like the breakfast you might have to prepare for the family, will require getting the consensus of everyone else. You may argue that that does not happen if you are alone, but even then, you will have to negotiate with yourself on the choices that you make for yourself.

So, if negotiation is that important in life, why should you not learn to employ the best of techniques to negotiate? The power of negotiating gives you the satisfaction of being considered important and gives you self-worth. This chapter is designed to provide you with a set of handy tactics you can use to be successful in your negotiation.

Six Golden Rules for Effective Negotiator

You may believe that the skill of negotiation is something that is innate for some and could be learned by others, but negotiation is not as complex as it seems. It is based on two fundamental aspects, logic and tact. The only problem is that you tend to camouflage these two aspects with all sorts of unwanted behavioral characteristics like ego that completely modifies them out of recognition. You do not want to get into an argument, and neither does anyone else. No one will have negative intentions, and you know that getting yourself into an unwanted scuffle over an issue that can be resolved amicably will only lead to you losing your mental peace. In an attempt to feel you are right or more importantly your opponent is wrong, you tend to forget that it would have been all the better to be able to say, "See, I told you." This is where you need to use negotiation to attain peace and thereby lasting success.

Rule 1 – Identifying Common Ground

First, you need to understand that for a negotiation to occur, you need to find common ground. Take a common situation like a family deciding on a restaurant. Every individual in the family might have a different favorite diner, but their common goal is to have a relaxed meal. Understanding this common goal will reduce the amount of sibling rivalry in deciding a feasible dining place that caters to everyone's needs.

To arrive at common ground, you have to think of ways to outline the negotiation so that you can work in partnership to resolve the problem. It's important to remember that your problem is not the person in front of you but the issue in question. You must keep in mind that you do not oppose your opponent, but his stance on the issue. You need to understand that in negotiation, the objective is never to create a winner and a loser but to create a win-win situation for both. You should realize that by wanting to achieve this, you are letting go of that competitive mentality that gives rise to unwanted body language, the undesirable tone in speech, and unwanted choices of words.

This will open doors to realizing the basic goals that you might want to work on in collaboration to meet the common core issue. This will also lead you to be open to others' rationales on the issue and will take you forward to the next step as proposed by Joseph O'Connor and John Seymour in their book *"Stepping Up"*.

Rule 2 – Stepping Up

The next step in negotiating would be for you to step up. In stepping up, the intention is to identify smaller goals as stepping-stones to achieving a larger goal. For instance, let us say that your ultimate goal is to get an advanced degree in some particular field. You will have to break down your larger goal into smaller, much more manageable goals, such as finding a school whose curriculum and timetables fit your learning requirements and busy schedule.

By stepping up in a negotiation, you see the bigger picture, tend to generalize intentions, and will be able to identify more options in solving the issue than just one non-compromising option. Another benefit of stepping up is that it almost always reminds you that the objective behind the disagreement is not the disagreement at all but is linked to something broader and common to both parties. Therefore, it is very important that when a disagreement arises that you step up before the quarrel evolves, leaving both sides in distress.

Rule 3 – Never Retort

The next technique that you need to keep in mind is never to retort. When an idea is suggested, it means that the person providing the idea had to invest in a lot of thinking before it was suggested. This would mean that they would be highly sensitive to any opposition that is likely to come their way. The best way to negotiate it through would be to give it some time, look at it from their perspective, and consider if the suggested idea has any sort of credibility. Instead of disapproving outright, it is better to show them the flaws of their proposal than to tell them. People tend to believe only through personal experience. Later explaining your position will make more sense than it would have, had you retorted in the beginning, and they will automatically see your reasons as to why you disagreed in the beginning.

Rule 4 – Questioning

Questioning the opposition in a respectful manner is the next important step in effective negotiation. If you find a flaw in the person's proposition, then phrase a question which will make the person realize his flaw. Instead of you stating it outright, which will only make the person defensive, intelligent questions are your negotiation weapons which can be used to break down the opposition's proposal in a polite manner while simultaneously leading them towards your idea.

The best possible manner to put forward a question is to request permission before it, such as "Will you mind answering some questions to satisfy my curiosity?" This will hike up your image and respect in the eyes of your opposition, not to mention that you will be guaranteed answers as they cannot elude responding to them once they have given consent.

Rule 5 – Hypothetical Scenario

If nothing we've discussed seems to be working for you, try guiding the opposition away from the negotiation. You can do this by cleverly changing the tracks of the discussion towards a hypothetical scenario by using persuasive speech such as "under what circumstances will you consent to my proposition?"

This will corner your opponent into stating the condition(s) which will assure you a successful negotiation, provided you can meet them. If you are a teenager who's seeking permission from your parents to attend the prom and aren't having any progress convincing them, try asking your parents what they would require from you in order to consent. This will force them to give you a response, which you can then use to gain what you want.

Rule 6 – Resist Intimation

Learn the art of turning the tables on your opponent. This is necessary only if you are ridiculed for your stance. For instance, if you have proposed an idea that is totally off the wall and inconsistent with the others' suggestions, people are going to throw sarcastic comments at you to throw you off your feet. The most common phrases you might encounter include "Seriously? You would go ahead with such a plan?", or, "Really? Is that your justification for the whole situation?"

Normally what would happen is that you would try to scrabble together a different, more plausible explanation for your words. Refrain from doing so. Instead, be firm and stand your ground by responding calmly, "Yes, this is all I have to say", or, "Yes, you heard it right; that's my plan." This will throw your audience off their feet and get them scrambling for reasons to try and overthrow your suggestions. If you opt for the former reaction- trying to revise your idea to be more acceptable - you are only portraying a weak personality and an indecisive mind which will not hold in a negotiation.

Tools for Persuasion

How can you convince people that you are absolutely right in your stance? Below are two powerful tactics that you might argue are common habits in conversations yet could be used to steer the unconscious mind of your client, spouse, or any opponent to accept your idea without a doubt.

The good option vs. the really bad option

An effective way of putting forward your suggestion would be to exaggerate its benefits in contrast to an amplified negative alternative.

Take the above example of deciding on a place to dine with your family. You might want to eat healthily, so you suggest a vegan restaurant. Your siblings might want to eat junk, so they suggest burgers. Normally you would all shout out your individual choices until you get on your parents' nerves and then end up dining at a totally weird restaurant picked out by your dad.

Here's how you change the scene to your advantage. Remember that the way you frame your suggestion has a profound impact on the outcome of the negotiation. An effective way of putting forward your idea is to make a comparison between the available options by portraying your idea as the best option and highlighting the drawbacks of other options. For example, "Do you guys want to eat a wholesome meal at Calorie Counter or eat burgers and increase your chances of developing high cholesterol?"

This puts a spin on the negotiation because it is no longer a negotiation of diners alone, but an option between well-being and bad health choices. Try this tactic once, and you will see how effective it is.

View the available options in terms of hypothetical everyday events.

Compare your options to everyday events in life. This gives context to your negotiation by adding a new simpler dimension to the whole discussion. For example, when you are trying to decide between two dresses, one which costs $100 and another which costs $75, you are most likely to calculate how many days' savings are going to be invested in this one dress. Another way of looking at it will be to equate the cost to a daily expense of yours, which can be sacrificed for a short while. So instead of looking at the expensive dress as something that will cost you 2 months of saving, try to look at it as taking a tube to work instead of a taxi for one month (the saving will be the cost of your dress).

Similarly, you can use this tactic when you are trying to persuade someone to buy a costly product; for example, a food mixer. Instead of trying to engage in a never-ending bargain with your customers, it would be more effective to equate the usefulness of the product to efficiency and time-saving features which will appeal to clients.

Chapter Seven: Chapter Seven - Become a Social Influencer through NLP

Up to now, you have been reading about different NLP techniques which can be used to increase efficiency in communication within and between people. Now is the time to put it all in to practice and test to see if you have fully grasped the concepts. So how are you going to use the NLP skills you gathered to become a successful social influencer?

What Is Social Influence?

Social influence is the conscious or subconscious change in a person's behavior as a result of exposure to social pressures. So, if you are a social influencer and you are practicing NLP, you aim to cause a change in another's behavior by applying certain techniques of NLP.

It would be helpful to study prominent social influencers of today and observe the methods they utilize to gain the compliance of their audiences. Consider the example of the Internet. The Internet is the largest form of communication in the world, which influences every individual even if they are not a direct user of the Internet. Other social influencers include politicians who are constantly campaigning to try and persuade people to elect them to power. So how do you go about being a social influencer on the Internet?

How to Influence on the Internet

Here are some useful tips which will assure you a large number of supporters:

- Portray yourself as a multi-dimensional character. People love change, and a personality with many angles stirs their curiosity, which will keep them tuned to your performance.

- Identify your strengths and use them to your advantage. Recognize which of your traits capture the attention of your audience (for example, good looks or a compelling voice). Use these qualities wisely so as to appear humble and connect to the audience instead of flaunting yourself, which will make you arrogant in the eyes of your followers.

- Connect with your audience. Present yourself in a seemingly approachable manner so that you share some common ground with the public. If people can relate to you, you stand a higher chance of being a part of their circle of influence.

- Emotion – the single effective instrument which will secure a place in the mind of your audience. Do not hesitate or be afraid to show emotions as this only makes you more human and allows you to reach your spectators at a primal level.

- Be realistic. Present your case in a realistic manner instead of trying to promise the entire universe, which is not something you can achieve.

- Use a reinforcement system where your audience has something to gain by supporting you. This will create a sense of hope, which will encourage them to stay tuned to you.

- Pay attention to feedback – use the criticisms that are directed your way to curb and reform yourself. If you want to be a successful social influencer, you need to become the person the public seeks. Only then can you gain their support.

- Build suspense - create a sense of anticipation which will leave the audience longing for your next performance. This is the tactic used in TV serials, where each episode ends in a cloud of suspense.

Using NLP to Become a Successful Social Influencer

In doesn't matter on what scale you wish to influence, be it the masses or a single individual; whether you are a mum who wants to have a positive influence on her kids or someone who wants to seal a multimillion-dollar deal, you need to be able first to reach your audience. This chapter is dedicated to training you to adapt qualities that will help you connect with and influence your audience successfully.

Here are a few handy rules of **NLP**, which you can keep in mind while trying to persuade someone.

1) It's easier to change your perception of reality than to change reality.

This is an extrapolation to what you learned in Chapter Two on "Framing and Reframing". In chapter two, you read about how events, in reality, have no meaning other than that attached to them. At a particular moment in life, you are bombarded with millions of sensory stimuli in the form of sights, sounds, smells, and tactile sensations; however, you only choose to focus your attention on selective stimuli, and this focus of yours defines the meaning of that reality to you.

Points to remember:

- There is no static reality
- Every individual has their own perception of reality.

When you are seated in a lecture hall you can hear the lecturer, observe all the people seated around you, hear the sounds of vehicles passing by, feel the temperature of the room, etc. Still, you choose to ignore everything and only focus on what is being discussed in the lecture. While you may sum up your experience as the content of the lecture, someone else who slept through the lecture will have a different perception of the lecture.

2) When you are communicating, it is your responsibility to control the other person's reaction.

A common misconception is that what you say is what the other person hears. Well, it's not always that simple. It may be true if you are talking to your clone or someone who is in total rapport with you because you both are thinking and talking on the same wavelength. However, most often you are trying to persuade and influence someone who is not in sync with you. So, what you say is not the same information that gets registered in their minds. It's their perception of what you say that gets recorded.

Have you ever had an instance in life when you said something neutral like "Honey, your cooking tastes different today," and your spouse just jumps your case and retorts "You're so ungrateful! Always complaining about my culinary skills!", and you stare in surprise, wondering what triggered this sudden outburst.

So how do you go about controlling the perceptions of others when communicating?

You achieve this by taking responsibility for the reaction of the other person to your statement. Instead of saying what you would like to say, you take a moment to analyze the situation and say what the other person wants to hear in their own language. To do this, you have to study the person, their levels of sensitivity, their emotions, body language, facial expressions, beliefs, etc. and gain a complete understanding of their thought processes before attempting to influence them. You need to empathize with people to be persuasive.

The next time you want to compliment your wife's cooking, figure out her mood and communicate your opinion straightforwardly by saying "Honey, your cooking is simply delicious today!" instead of being vague and leaving room for misunderstandings. A neutral statement can be analyzed in both a positive and negative manner.

Realizing this fact, that people might require something different than what you have to say, is vital for gaining influential power over another. If you can deliver what the person seeks from you in communication, you are bound to be successful in your aim of directing the person towards your goal.

Go back to the premise from Chapter Four on "Anchoring", which stated that people associate with those who are similar to them. Aren't these ideas overlapping?

So, if you can empathize with and sound similar to your audience by speaking to them in a language that they can understand, you stand a higher chance of influencing them. This is why you find political leaders addressing different issues in different locales. Their main aim is to win the support of the public, but they don't to it by explicitly asking people to support them. Instead, they go campaigning, where they highlight certain persistent issues in rural locales. This is a method of putting across your message in a manner that is acceptable to your audience. By addressing problems of the masses, they appear to be shouldering their worries and, by doing so, bridging the gap between them, which gives the politicians an edge in gaining the support of the public.

3) Human behavior is always rational.

Yet another extrapolation from Chapter Two states that there is a positive intention motivating every behavior, and in some context, every behavior has value.

Acknowledging this principle of NLP makes you open-minded and is extremely helpful when you analyze the purpose of another person's behavior. So even if someone does something which might seem bizarre or unacceptable to you, you still try to find out the positive intent governing the whole action. Interestingly, you might find out that the person stole food did so to feed his starving family, which sheds a lot of light on the situation when you try to influence and guide the person towards a more productive solution. There are essentially no "bad people" in society, and by highlighting the positive intentions of people they can come to view themselves more favorably, which extends to their being susceptible to positive alternatives suggested by themselves or an external source.

Capturing the Mind of the Audience

To be able to persuade an audience, you need to be able to GRIP their minds and direct it to where you want it to be. Many of the techniques used in NLP are carried out unconsciously, and one might argue that all these techniques are a matter of simple common sense. But unfortunately, common sense isn't very common. So, here is the GRIPS method of applying common sense to your daily communications, which will enable you to hold the mind of the person and guide it towards your goal.

- Gather intelligence (G)

What is the first thing you need to do before you start a task?

You need to collect information about the job.

Social influencing is no different. You need to gather information about your audience before you approach them initially. Information regarding your opponent can be in the form of their preconceived notions as well as real-time facts such as body posture, facial expressions, fashion, etc. Putting together a mental portfolio about your audience will help you recognize what sort of approaches will be acceptable and what should be avoided. It's similar to point 2 mentioned above, which is where you study your audience so that you can ensure you put forward your message in a manner they expect to hear.

- Reduce resistance (R)

People are naturally programmed to resist any attempt of persuasion. It's a type of defense mechanism which your body engages in to repel all forms of influence and maintain the original views of the self. As an effective social influencer, your task is to break this natural barrier erected by the self and reach the person's mind. You can easily achieve this through rapport, which was discussed in detail in Chapter Three.

- Induce control (I)

People only resist influence on a conscious level. An alternative route to manipulating individuals is by targeting the subconscious mind. You can do this by using automatic triggers to which the mind is programmed to react. A common premise of the human mind is that it must do more to avoid the loss of something than to gain something. Ever heard the proverb, "Absence makes the heart grow fonder?" So, if you can introduce the scarcity trigger by connecting your message to a loss of something which matters to your audience, you've managed to activate the subconscious mind, which will assure you that your message gets registered at a core level.

- Position (P)

Refers to the image of yourself in the mind of your audience. People construct mental images of others, depending on the purpose served by their relationship. In other words, people choose to be in the company of others either to gain something, protect themselves from losing something, or simply for entertainment. Therefore, it is your responsibility to position yourself as the best candidate for whichever purpose you wish to serve.

- Sustain the position (S)

Once you have established your position in the mind of the audience, it is necessary to maintain that position by keeping in contact with them over time. You cannot become a social influencer in simply one encounter. It's a skill that requires time and consistency.

Following up your supporters or clientele either through messages or calls will ensure that you are frequently remembered, thereby strengthening your position in their minds.

Chapter Eight: Transformative NLP for Positivity and Confidence

NLP for Positivity and Confidence

The first term in "Neuro-Linguistic Programming" relates to how your mind activates neurons when you are in the process of learning. It is significant to keep in mind that training your mind by learning something can be either positive or negative. You can either learn something that can have a positive impact on your life, or you can also learn something that can have a negative impact on your life.

The next term, "linguistic," is used in regard to how language plays a tremendous role in constructing reality. The terms we use in our language have a huge impact on how we perceive the world around us.

Next in line is "Programming" which states that all of us have been programmed by the languages that we use and the beliefs that we hold.

The entire concept declares that by modifying our beliefs and language we can reconstruct ourselves into better human beings. You can make positive changes in your life. You can boost your level of confidence and eliminate negative values and beliefs that are negatively influencing you. The goals that you set and the path you travel can be consciously picked up by you.

Boost your Positivity with NLP

As humans, we are structured in such a way that we tend to pay more attention to the negative rather than the positive. How do we train ourselves to overcome this negativity? Training our mind to positivity and positive thinking is not as complicated as you may think; it is simply a matter of reconstructing your unconscious mind. To lead your life with positivity, you must believe that good things will happen instead of always believing that the worst might take place.

You need to take control of a few things to be more positive

1. Believe that every behavior or action holds a positive intention: by training your mind to do this, it will be easy for you to deal with any type of human being.

2. Pay attention to everything that is around you with all the senses that you have: try to pay attention to more positive things rather than negatives and record them on something that you can review before ending the day. Try to be more conscious and mindful of what's going on in your head. Ask yourself questions, is it useful? Is it going to help me? And never forget to appreciate things that make you feel good.

3. Develop elasticity in selecting what you choose to pay attention to. Keep in mind the more flexible you are, the more positive results you get because when you can change your behavior, you will be able to change your thoughts. We also need to omit things that cause disruption.

4. Try to place yourself in someone else's position: by allowing your mind to do this, you will be able to get along with the ones which cause you discomfort.

5. Look for role models who spread positivity: take notice of things that these individuals do and how do they maintain their qualities.

6. Assemble rapport: you don't necessarily need to love everyone you meet, but to keep your mind in a positive state have empathy towards everyone.

7. The body and mind vs negative emotions: remember that your body and your mind are always interconnected; to keep them both healthy you need to move away from your negative emotions. Hold on to positive emotions and the emotions that give you comfort.

8. Do actions. Get up, smile, give yourself a pat; these actions will induce physiological changes that have a tremendous impact on your mental health.

NLP Trains You to Gain Confidence

NLP is a significant tool that is handled by practitioners and trainers to guide you to gain and strengthen your confidence. This confidence is just the same as the confidence that is gained through real-life experiences. Although confidence is something that can be gained through different techniques, most of us lack this ability due to past experiences that have taken place in our lives. Confidence is not about feeling proud of yourself by putting others in a lower position, but the courage to hold yourself higher each time something happens.

The following scenario presents a negative confidence cycle.

Current situation: *I am going to sit for my exams. What are my feelings regarding this?*

Memory: *Last time I failed in my exams. I'm going to fail this time also, and my classmates are going to make fun of me.*

Emotions: *I'm not going to let this happen again. Oh my god, I'm worried.*

Neuro-physical effects: *Anxiousness and inability to relax.*

The next scenario presents a positive confidence cycle.

Current situation: *I am going to face my exams.*

Memory: *Last time I passed my exams, and I was happy. My classmates appreciated me.*

Emotions: *I gained good results last time and loved the feeling of being passed in my exams.*

Neuro physical effects: *Feels good, happy, and excited.*

The following are some techniques put forward by NLP to strengthen and gain confidence.

1. Avoid holding confidence in awe.

If you're a person who is trying to hold on to confidence with concern and panic, then your mind is going to make you feel like confidence is something that is hard to handle. You need to train your mind to understand that confidence is a small thing that is easy to handle.

2. Imagine your confidence as golden aura around you.

Imagine yourself being an extremely confident individual; people are going to love you because you fear nothing, you walk and talk with confidence.

3. Sense how it makes you feel to be 100% confident both in the known and unknown setting.

Believe in yourself and pay attention to a memory in which you were 100% confident.

4. Move forward to the future.

Have you ever thought of a situation that is going to bring up an argument in the future, and that made you feel irritated and angry? Why don't you imagine the same situation with a positive outcome? By training your mind to get a positive outcome, you will be able to fix your mind to gain positive outcomes.

5. Alter your self-talk.

Pay close attention to where the negative voice is coming from. Is it on the right side of your head? Left side? Where is it? Now try to change the voice that makes you feel uneasy; give it a nice voice, try to change what the voice says, and move the location from which the voice is coming. This technique can help reduce these negative thoughts about yourself.

6. Imagine yourself.

Imagine yourself being confident in the situation in which you think you will not have enough confidence. Even if this is imagination, your mind will not be able to differentiate between reality and imagination. This technique helps you boost your confidence level.

Powerful Tool to Get Rid of Anxiety

Anxiety is the body's automatic and innate response that occurs due to the stress that you go through. It also can be described as the sensation of fear and worry about something in the future. Anxiety is of different types which are classified according to the degree to which anxiety takes place. One of the most powerful tools that are used to guide individuals with anxiety is **NLP**.

1. Keep "you" on top of the priority list.

Give yourself enough time. One of the most negative things that we do is forgetting to treat ourselves; this can be unhealthy. To treat yourself, you need to begin your day by doing something that you like, such as dancing, jogging, listening to music, etc. By doing this, you can non-verbally shout out to the world that you are always the first on your list.

2. Keep in mind the feeling that triggers your anxiety.

Fantasize the event or the person that causes the feeling of anxiety in you, pay attention to it closely as you can. Notice where the pain in your body is when you start feeling anxious. Is it in your stomach? Your chest? Your hands? Where is it? Pay attention to how these feelings are unstable; they don't stay still. They keep moving from one place to the other. Notice this unstable pain and try to make it move faster. At the initial stage, you are going to feel pain and suffering, but that is a good sign; it signifies that you control yourself and that an outside event is not controlling you.

3. Give this unstable ball of pain a color.

Give this mobile ball a red color and now take notice of the direction that the ball is moving. Now try to take this object outside your body and pay attention to it. Make the ball into a blue color through your imagination and change its direction of moving. Visualize this blue ball moving in the opposite direction into your body. Now take notice of the movement of the ball, you will notice that this movement gives you a different feeling, a feeling that is way much better than the feeling that you went through before. Imagine something that makes you feel good and gives your comfort; pay attention to how it makes you feel, and then mix this feeling of comfort with the blue object that is spinning in you. Pay attention to everything that is around you, including your breathing. Now relax and calm yourself.

4. Think of good things before bed.

Don't allow yourself to think of things that have negatively impacted you or seem problematic to you. Thinking of something that negatively affects you before going to bed makes you more stressed, worried, and anxious. Try to end your day by thinking and feeling things that cause positive responses in your body.

By training your mind to increase positivity and boost your confidence, you will be able to increase the level of esteem you have about yourself. You will be an individual who perceives yourself and others more optimistically. By following these techniques, you will be able to develop into an individual with empathy. You will be able to face real-life situations with strength, power, and confidence, which will help you to lead a more productive and successful life.

Chapter Nine: Success NLP: Get What You Want NOW

Have you ever had a time in life when you didn't know what you wanted? Or you wanted something, but were not able to achieve it? Or you simply didn't know how to achieve it?

Everyone experiences setbacks in life at some point or another. People don't always end up achieving all their dreams. There are moments in life when people are forced to face reality and reset their goals. The differences between people lie in their reactions to these setbacks. Some people can pick themselves up and walk again while some others lay fallen for longer. So how do you react when you are confronted with such a situation? Your reaction will determine the outcome of the event.

Have you ever wondered why you weren't able to achieve your goal? Have you ever wondered how someone else managed to reach the same goal which you failed to achieve? Does that suggest that there is a secret ingredient to success? Or is a success a result of chance?

Yes, there is a secret ingredient to success, and success is not a function of mere chance. The only reason why you haven't been able to succeed still is that you are unaware or ignorant of the secrets to success. In fact, you already possess the ingredient, so it's only a matter of tapping into it the next time you try to achieve your goal.

Here's how you're going to get it right this time. In the past, you may have tried countless times and not achieved your dreams, but this time you have a tool you can use to succeed – NLP.

This chapter is designed to help you use NLP techniques effectively in reaching your goals in life. The ultimate formula for success is gaining control of your mind and using that to design your destiny. It lies in believing in yourself and your capability to achieve what you want. Success can be attained if you step out of or break the vicious cycle of failure that surrounds you and replace those feelings of inadequacy and hopelessness with determination and positive self-talk.

The Components of NLP

Let's break down NLP into its subcomponents and try to identify how this tool can be used to produce results in your life.

"Neuro" refers to an individual's nervous system, which links the brain to your body. Thoughts and emotions are generated by your mind, which is essentially your brain. So, according to NLP, since your brain and body are linked, you should be able to control your thoughts and emotions which will in turn affect your actions.

A common problem in people is that they lack control over their thoughts and emotions. Most people allow emotions to drive them, which results in people losing control over their lives. So, if you can master the technique of controlling your mind, you can gain control over your life and direct yourself towards achieving your goals.

According to NLP, every individual shares the same neurobiology. Therefore, if someone else can achieve something, there is no reason why you cannot do the same. It's a matter of which strategy you use which will determine if you reach your goal or not.

So, take the first step towards changing your perception of reality by understanding that there is nothing that you cannot achieve (provided that it is something that has been achieved by another person).

"Linguistic" means language or communication. In NLP terms, it refers to the effect of language on thoughts and emotions, which affect actions and outcomes. NLP focuses on two types of communications: interpersonal and intrapersonal. While the first few chapters of this book concentrated on enhancing interpersonal communication styles (interactions between people), this specific chapter emphasizes on intrapersonal communication (interaction within the individual).

Are you surprised to hear that you talk with yourself? For those of you who have doubts, yes, you definitely do talk to yourself daily. Self-talk is a primary mode of communicating with yourself. Self-talk can be either positive or negative. If you are going to ask yourself, "Why me?", or say to yourself, "This always happens to me" and "I can't achieve anything in life", you are installing negative thoughts into yourself, which is going to initiate a vicious cycle of depressive thoughts. Instead, if you use positive talk like "How can I use this opportunity to make myself better?", or "What do I have to learn from this setback in life?", reframing it will help to create a new experience.

Identify what type of self-talk you use on yourself and alter it accordingly if it is negative.

"Programming" in NLP refers to conditioning yourself over time to develop certain habits by repetitively exposing yourself to the same stimuli. So, if you program yourself by constantly feeding positive, motivational thoughts and beliefs into your system, then with time, you will only feel positive vibes, which will result in a healthy, productive mind. But if you constantly associate negativity to circumstances, then you condition your mind to become unhealthy, and an unhealthy mind is unproductive.

Ask yourself, "What are the programs that run my life?" and reprogram any unhealthy habits that govern your actions. Using NLP

Anchoring, recondition your fears and replace them with confidence; replace laziness with motivation, doubt with certainty, and hopelessness with determination.

If you can gain proficiency in effective communication between your mind and body, gain control of your thoughts and emotions, understand the language of your mind, and install productive programs to run your life, then you are just a step away from getting what you want.

The Three Steps to Success

The path to success can be condensed into three simple steps.

1) Set precise and clear goals.

Identify what it is that you want in life. A common problem among the majority of people is that they do not know what exactly they want in life. They might be able to state what they don't want clearly, but their ideas of their goals are vague.

Take responsibility for your destiny and identify what exactly you want to be in the future. Don't wait for opportunities to come knocking on your door. You create them yourself by designing your ecology. No goal is unachievable if you believe. It's all a matter of perception. If you program yourself to believe that you are capable of improving, then there is nothing to stop you from being who you want to be.

Employ yourself. If you don't pursue your goals in life, then someone else will employ you to pursue their goals. Therefore, it's a matter of deciding whose goal is a priority to you.

2) Strategy

There are specific behaviors and schedules necessary to reach certain goals. For instance, if your goal is to lose twenty kilograms in six months, then there is a detailed diet plan that you have to follow to lose a certain percentage of weight every month, which will finally give you your results at the end of six months.

Planning your strategy is vital to success. Failing to plan is planning to fail.

If you can't design a feasible plan by yourself, model the behavior of those who have achieved similar goals to yours. You can be assured that if you follow the path of the previously successful, it will lead you to the same destination.

3) Consistent action

Transform your goal into an obsession that you work towards every single day. Do something daily, no matter how insignificant it may be, to take you closer to your goal. The biggest secret to success in life is to take action. It might sound like a really simple step, but how many times have you procrastinated instead of acting? The answer is practically every day! And why do you procrastinate? Because you don't feel like taking action.

So how do you combat this feeling of yours, which is holding you back from progressing?

Anchoring, described in Chapter 3, will provide you instantaneous results.

Once you take action, you get results. Results are of two types – favorable and unfavorable. The majority of the time, the results are unfavorable because chances that you master the strategy to success on the first attempt are highly unlikely. You will be surprised to find that truly successful people have faced numerous failures; the secret is not to be afraid of failure.

So how do you react in the face of unfavorable results?

You can:

i) Give up

ii) Try again

iii) Consider your failure as feedback and change your strategy and try again.

The third option, by far, is the most productive choice. The first two options won't yield positive results because giving up or trying numerous times with the same strategy will only produce the same results: loss. To be victorious in life, you have to be flexible and change your approach towards the task until you find the correct rhythm, which gives you the expected results.

Remember that the three steps mentioned above are sequential. So, if one step doesn't work out, you go back to the previous step and resume the process once again.

What Is the Driving Force in Life?

Have you ever experienced a time in your life when you were highly motivated to achieve something, but after some time you felt demotivated in pursuing the goal?

Often, it is because as you age your interests and priorities in life change. So, what you aim for as a teenager is not the same goal as when you become an entrepreneur. For example, as a typical teenager, your goal in life would be to top your class and become famous. But once you hit your thirties and you have your own business, topping your class or becoming famous is no longer on your list of needs. Instead, your goal would be to become financially stable or buy a penthouse.

But irrespective of age and interests, how do you get back your high levels of energy that you suddenly lose while trying to achieve your goal?

When you feel like quitting, remember why you started. Your purpose in achieving your goal serves as fuel for your actions. Your beliefs, morals, and values surrounding your goals drive you to achieve them. So, think back to why you initially wanted to reach a particular goal. Reviving those thoughts will rekindle your spirit and reawaken the energy inside of you, fueling your actions so that once again you can target your goal. If you're a businessman who has experienced an unexpected loss, you may feel demotivated and hopeless. You may be on the verge of selling off your business because you believe it's unrecoverable. Take a moment to think back to why you initially invested in the business. Does it hold a sentimental value for you, or are you serving humanity through your services? A moment of introspection might save your lifelong efforts.

The Biggest Enemy

Have you ever wondered who you are up against in life? You are your biggest enemy in achieving your dreams. Obstacles in life will only prevent you from progressing if you view them as negativity. Negativity only stems from within you. If you are someone who believes that circumstances in life, destiny, or the comments and actions of others deter you from reaching your goals, then this information is for you.

Understand that you are responsible for your destiny and the results of your actions. It's all a matter of perception when you perceive an unfavorable outcome as a failure. Remember that failure is only an illusion of the mind, which can be transformed into an opportunity using NLP reframing.

If you are the businessman who has faced a loss, then win the battle with your mind and transform the loss into an opportunity for learning what shouldn't be done in business. This will enable you to grow as an individual and take you to higher standards in your career.

The Law of Identity and Factors that Influence Your Identity

Your identity is dependent on your ecosystem and internal pillars. The law of identity states that what you see in yourself is what you will create for yourself in life.

If you take a moment to ponder over this law, you will realize that you are the sole designer of your destiny. You hold the secrets to your success. Your vision of yourself becomes your reality. So, the next time you feel hopeless, just look at yourself in the mirror, identify the reflection, and determine if that person is who you want to be.

Your identity is grounded on four pillars: psychology, physiology, history, and philosophy. Psychology refers to how your mind works, physiology is your body postures and facial expressions, your history consists of your past experiences, and your philosophy includes your beliefs and values. These four factors intersect with each other creating an illusion that affects your identity and perception of reality. Who you are depends on your past, your current belief system, your physical self, and your manner of processing information.

So, when you start intervening with yourself, remember that changing one factor will cause a change in another pillar. So, keep fine-tuning until you find the perfect synchrony which will support your identity. For example, if you are confronted with business failure, your reaction to it will depend on whether you have previously incurred such losses, your physical reaction, your perception of the loss, and your underlying belief regarding this circumstance. If you wish to change your perception, then you have to let go of your past experiences, challenge your beliefs, and replace your frown with a smile.

Your ecology consists of your social, internal, and physical environment.

If you can tailor your ecosystem and anchor in your identity, then you can be sure of having control and being goal-oriented in your actions.

You might argue that you don't have control over ecology. Even though it may be true, you still have control over strategy. And you can create change if you learn the art of hijacking your mind and rewiring it. You can achieve this only if you have an identity within you which you can depend on.

Believe that success is possible. Understand the correlation between your internal and external environments. If you can create change in your internal environment, then producing a change in the external environment is simple. So instead of focusing your efforts on changing external circumstances in life, which will not yield results if your internal environment is not healthy, concentrate on altering your inner self, which will guarantee you victory.

Part 3: Dark NLP

Chapter Ten: Is NLP a Form of Manipulation?

In this chapter, we will be getting into the dark side of NLP and how its techniques are employed by manipulators, liars, and deceivers for their own gain. These tactics can, however, also be applied by people who just want to sell a product, get promoted, or pursue some other less reprehensible cause. Hence, do not paint NLP in an entirely negative light. The chapter explains how NLP as a tool helps people for their personal gain or everyday goals.

What is Manipulation?

Manipulation, by the dictionary's definition, is the process of skillfully controlling (or influencing) a situation, a subject, or set of events with the intention of utilizing it for your own gain.

Where manipulation has been cultivated, accepted, and ingrained in a culture, it is worth mentioning that NLP does have a shared history with that culture.

That is explicitly why the ethics involved in using NLP are in the grey area and often difficult to navigate. Where does a teacher draw the line between motivating failing students to do better and ruthlessly eroding students' mental health for the sake of keeping the average grade percentage high? When is a therapist toeing the line between changing a trauma victim's psychological map of the world and programming the century's most infamous shooter?

The answer may seem elusive but in the end it all boils down to a simple thing: the individual's intention.

How to Use NLP as a Useful Tool to Manipulate

Your intentions are the only North Star in a dark and lonely ocean. It is the only thing that sets NLP apart from manipulation by serving as a useful tool to remember the actual purpose of using NLP. Studies show that when innately aware of your goals, your brain subtly works towards achieving them, even when you aren't actively thinking about it. It is known as "diffused thinking" when you allow your mind to wander freely, making connections at random. It's a process that encompasses all parts of the brain and is commonly used to solve problems and difficult concepts. The true motive can sit undisturbed, deep in your subconscious, while your brain works around it, trying to come up with ways and plans to achieve it. NLP is a set of skills that allows you as the user to be in control of your own conscious and unconscious mind.

However, that doesn't mean that NLP is unsuccessful if the user's intentions are immoral. It is possible to imbue those habits that were known to be practiced by historically unsavory characters such as criminals and terrorists; thus, the patient can be fashioned into the next revolutionary terrorist who ushers in a new era, or even completely reinvents modern violence as we know it. This is an example of the most extreme cases. More subtle manipulation, the kind that may not make headlines and morning news, can be equally deadly.

For example, consider this hypothetical scenario between two rival law firms, both competing for the same large client. Law firm 'A' plans to manipulate the client's choice by presenting their rival law firm in a bad light. This is done by hiring a programmer to sit in on the regular therapy sessions of Law firm 'B's top attorney and subtly twist the patient's view of his/her relationship with their spouse, planting subconscious suggestions of problems in the relationship that do not exist. This technique would fall under the category of manipulation in court, with or without the use of NLP.

Another instance of manipulation your brain doesn't commonly recognize because humans are sympathetic creatures is the emotional manipulation done by beggars. Though there is a percentage of 'honest' beggars, who are truly homeless and struggling to survive, there is an astounding majority of those whose trade is begging.

It is quite popular in the South Asian region, and the manipulators often don patchy clothes and have dirty faces. They use words and behaviors to play on the emotions to try to convince people that they need money. Many even go the extra mile and hire children for the day, just to rub it in. The manipulation is done so well that whether they have trained themselves in NLP techniques or not, they are very good at it.

On the other hand, NLP programmers hired to hold regular workshops in businesses (such as our hypothetical law firms, for instance) use it as a tool to help boost employee motivation, and encourage them to pick up new skill-sets that have been attributed to highly successful individuals, in a bid to improve general worker productivity and employee attitude in the company. It is a technique that has shown positive results.

Similarly, as it is used in business purposes to inspire workers, it is also commonly employed by a door-to-door salesman to sell as many products as possible and earn higher commissions.

Personal programmers work with their clients to help them repair relationships with their friends and family, helping to rectify and solve conflicts. NLP is also clinically utilized in curing mental illnesses like PTSD, GAD, phobias, anxieties, paranoia, and even substance misuse.

There are many more instances where NLP is employed, for good and bad, but the prevailing truth of the matter is that NLP itself is not guilty.

Like any technique or product, there are users and abusers.

The thing being (ab)used is innocent of the crime of the (ab)user. It's the abusers of NLP with immoral, nefarious motives that have brought a bad name on the personal development and psychotherapy technique so well-intended by Brandler and Grinder.

Chapter Eleven: The Kind Manipulator

Manipulation Techniques That Aren't So Bad!

This chapter elaborates on a few important NLP manipulation techniques that could be used to subtly manipulate someone to gain something positive or direct someone who might need a little push.

Many of us cannot deny that we have been tempted to use manipulation at different instances during our lifetime; whether it was telling a little lie to get out of a bad or embarrassing situation, using flattery and flirting to sell a product or get our way, we have all used manipulation to try to get what we want. Yet we would not categorize that as being intentionally harmful or abusive to the cause or the person, given that at the time of doing so, we thought it to be the best-suited course of action for the issue at hand. The outcome of this result may have been to our benefit or in the best interest of the other individual or both parties. But calling someone a manipulator is criticizing that person's character. Human nature is naturally inclined to be manipulative because we are always trying to influence one another at any given time.

If you try to force or mislead people to get what you want, they will eventually figure it out. Lying and misleading are short-term achievements: they don't build trust or form beneficial relationships. When you view NLP from a positive light, its singular purpose can be justified as a worthy cause.

NLP is a multi-dimensional process that contains a progression of collaborative capabilities and methods, careful thinking, and an understanding of the emotional and rational processes involved in human behavior. As such, it offers a set of tools and skills used for the development of the varied phases of individual excellence.

This sort of level-by-level building is the real secret to "getting someone to do what we want," but that is putting it crudely. When the person we want to influence is not only the other person but ourselves as well, this kind of endeavor can have a ton of fruitful results that are often forgotten among the darker and mysterious forms of NLP, or "manipulation."

Remember the three basic factors in NLP's name?

"Neuro" – the process of understanding the use of your senses by feeling, seeing, hearing, smell, and taste. Our nervous system processes our understanding of the world around us through the experiences of our senses.

"Linguistic" – our mental process of understanding is transferred and given meaning using language. How we communicate to ourselves and others around us is the system through which we make sense of our experiences.

"Programming" – the way you plan your ideas and actions in achieving your goals and specific outcomes through the result of your behavior.

How does one use a combination of these three factors to help unlock unlimited possibilities in ourselves and others? How does one overcome fear and painful memories, get rid of bad habits, beat depression and anxiety, adopt new habits, have better behavior and manners, improve social skills, gain accomplishments, be a better salesman and become a better communicator? This is where NLP techniques come in handy.

Using NLP techniques requires much training and practice. But there are some easy methods that you can use in your daily encounters. Be they friendships, family relationships, and romantic encounters or professional relationships, the relationships in our lives can be without a doubt be complicated. They can either enrich our lives or make them unbearable. As long as you are not using these methods to hurt people, this isn't such a bad thing. The essence of this is the intention, as mentioned in the previous chapter.

Let us look at some methods that have been recommended by advocates of this study:

1. Recommending scientific research and study on the topic. Making factual statements encourages a person to give you a listening ear. It will make what you say seem more valid.

Say you want to encourage a loved one who has diabetes to adopt healthier food and lifestyle changes. If you mention an extensive study or proven research that was conducted by a reputed university, they are more likely to listen to you.

2. Using reverse psychology or negative commands which prompt specific thoughts when you state the exact opposite of what you mean. This works especially well with young children. The conventional method of working with children in early childhood learning is to prevent and correct "wrong" behavior that could result in the child causing harm to themselves or others.

Imagine after having commanded your toddler not to slide down the staircase railing because of the danger of injuring himself, you then, out of annoyance, anger or desperation ask him to keep climbing and sliding until he falls and breaks his leg. Then, you continue, he can't ride his bicycle at the park that very same evening where you have planned an outing with his playmates. In a fit of childish rebellion, he is most likely to avoid the stairs in order to enjoy the outing with his friends.

3. Using a varying tone of voice and facial expressions is a powerful method if used appropriately. Have you noticed how our voice ends on a high note at the end of a question and how it is at a low note when we make a statement or when we make commands? The same applies to when we want to win an argument or convince someone.

4. Creating a rapport or connecting with another to make them like you. This requires a subtle emulating of the other person's body language, tone of voice, and words. It must be mirrored without making it too obvious, or it becomes creepy. Setting the same tone of the conversation, e.g., smiling the same way, crossing your legs or tilting your head when the other person does, and mirroring their emotions.

5. Anchoring is another NLP technique; it entails using images, words, or gestures from an emotional memory to trigger a specific feeling such as the feeling of achievement, of happiness, or of overcoming fears or uneasiness. You can use this on yourself or apply it to others.

6. Using an opportune moment to offer help or support to gain their trust or to "trap" them to feel committed to you so that you may achieve your goal.

For example, you might be a door-to-door salesman at the end of an unsuccessful day of trying to convince busy homemakers to buy a cable TV package, and you end up at the door of a lonely, elderly lady who wouldn't mind the few minutes of your company just to hear what you have to say. But as you get friendly and inquire about her day, you find out she is preparing food, but not able to complete the task herself, and so you offer to assist her. Seeing your good nature, she agrees. She then feels obliged to return the favor by purchasing your cable TV package. You were successful in the day's sale, and perhaps this customer may recommend you to others, thereby opening opportunities for more sales.

It is also largely used in the business world to motivate and inspire employees to perform better, achieve their target goals and improve productivity, allowing the opportunity to help them perform to their fullest potential. The positive result of this is that it is beneficial both to the employee and the employer.

For example, "company A" wishes to sell musical instruments to a large customer base; it needs to have a successful advertising campaign, an attractive package for the product, and a price that is psychologically appealing to the customer (in the way the prices of so many products are set below the whole number, for example, $9.99, easing the buyer's conscience knowing they didn't spend that extra buck). They also must consider appealing to the customer through images or playing out a story—much like the anchoring technique and strategies that would help influence human decisions using emotions.

NLP is used in advertising to convince the customer to look for products that are not on their wish-list. It gives the customer a false belief that they need to purchase this specific product. The task is a great one, having to convince a mass audience with varying preferences.

Knowing and understanding the darker techniques are beneficial; after all, it becomes difficult for someone to manipulate you if you recognize the methods. And learning about NLP will help you protect yourself from those who may want to take advantage of you or use your vulnerabilities to their benefit.

Sociopathic predators, narcissists, and psychopaths manipulate the NLP techniques to abuse a situation to their advantage and exploit the balance of power to serve their agenda. They can use happy memories and sabotage special events to make you feel threatened with horrific behavior. They can psychologically influence the more gullible of us into committing acts that are against our will or can use the "nice guy" act in an underhanded manner to get what they want regardless of the pain they may cause in the process. Such practices can be considered evil; NLP in the wrong hands can be dangerous or have disastrous outcomes.

Not all the above tips can be applied to a particular situation you may face, hence utilize what may work best for you. You mustn't violate the rights of others or cause harm to them by using NLP.

Chapter Twelve: NLP Techniques in Mass Mind Control (Media, Politics & Cults)

This chapter outline the techniques used by the media, advertising, politicians and governments, and cults to brainwash and manipulate the masses.

If we were all given the freedom to make our own choices, would this world be a better place? Does our individual choice benefit the collective? Since we are not able to do so collaboratively, others make choices for us.

The thought of "mind control" or brainwashing can stir different feelings within you. Would it be considered a violation of your most cherished God-given right – free will? You may have a subtle disinclination to the thought or entirely oppose it, whatever the nature of its use. Nevertheless, as with every other tool, mind-control techniques can be used for good or be abused for personal gain at the expense of others. Mass mind-control entails secret, sophisticated operations that have a major influence in our world, with the media taking center stage and using it as a tool for whoever controls it. Many of us are naïve when it comes to the destructive and disturbing nature of mind-controlling programs. Yet some who are aware of it may choose to ignore it (perhaps this is another type of mind control and not want to make the conscious effort to use their grey matter. Some are happy to let others do the thinking, thereby giving those in power free reign to cause more fear and divergence of our world. It is a rather common trend from companies to governments and everything in between to manipulate you into believing in something you do NOT believe in. For a long time, people have been in the dark, unaware of such a thing existing. But thanks to those who broke the code of silence to voice the injustice of such matters, today you have been made to open your eyes and minds. Sometimes those people are made to look like a rebel, like Julian Assange, Australian editor and publisher and the man behind WikiLeaks.

Due to the foundation already laid by the powers that be, we think the way we do because we are programmed to do so, and the rest that follows is the logical conclusion. Some components of dark NLP are possibly what is needed so that the elements of a collaborative society are firmly rooted, and a breakout of chaos and anarchy does not cause a nation to face irrevocable destruction.

Here are some of the areas where mass mind manipulation takes place.

Governments and Media

Can a democratically elected government operate to manipulate the willpower of the people? Throughout the history of our world, we have witnessed the rise of many powerful empires, regimes, and governments and their success at authoritative governing. Do elected governments rule with democracy? Mind control and brainwashing have long been used by governments all around the world. They use the media as their agent to convey the message. Politics and media have formed a great partnership in this powerful art of manipulation. They aim at sections of the population in different areas to address targeted problems that are relatable to them, re-framing their thoughts. They have the power to control the narrative in the news channels and newspapers. They can cause and solve nonexistent problems, they can distract the people from the problems that plague the world, and there will be no voice to rise and speak against them. Often, problems are created solely to create the demand for a solution where the government comes to the rescue. Manipulation at its finest!

A good example is a movie, *Wag the Dog* (1997), a comedy describing how the media can manipulate public opinion. What we can see from this movie is media using images and signs (NLP) to sidetrack (manipulate) the public's attention toward problems that may not apply to them. It shows us the power media can wield over the masses.

Governments allow controlled substances like liquor, anti-depressants, drugs, nicotine, and prescription drugs to control certain pockets of people so that they will not retaliate in ways that can affect the sociological balance.

The Freedom House President Michael Abramowitz stated that the use of paid critics and political forecasters to spread government propaganda has been established and become a global trend.

The fear factor is another way to make sure the nation is not allowed out of line. You create a cause to be feared, like an incurable disease or terrorist agents, and claim you are out on streets to monitor unscrupulous activities and those who aid the perpetrators. Conspiracy theorists often claim "false-flag" events are orchestrated with the use of crisis actors.

JAWS (1975) was one of the greatest films made; it was a high grossing movie until 1977. There was very little known about sharks during this time. The movie created a response of deep-rooted panic, fear, and terror resulting in beachgoers around the globe not patronizing even the safest of beaches. The media continues to stay committed to abuse that fear when the subject of sharks arises.

You are made fearful about which topics you can speak out about in public. You're made to be afraid of helping a stranger because you cannot be certain what his motive is. Will lending a helping-hand get you in trouble? You fear that your phone calls are being monitored. You constantly must watch your back.

Take North Korea, for instance. It remains the world's most oppressive country where the government continues to implement total political control of its society through fear, and where the activities of its people are monitored with an iron fist.

Advertising and Marketing

The art of persuasion has become a very profitable business in our times, with advertising playing the main role. You are continually being programmed and told what you must eat, what beauty products you should shop for, what insurance you must take up, what medical treatments you must follow, how you need to manage lifestyles and where you need to invest. The moment you switch on your TV, you are bombarded with commercials trying to convince you which product to buy.

Marketing is built on the principals of manipulation. The tactics used in magazines, billboards, posters, newspapers, free flyers, and television subconsciously tease you because your mind is absorbing all that information. If you see them enough times, you will feel a need for the products. Most marketers unethically manipulate their target audience, creating a sense of attachment to the product. Marketers don't just manipulate adults; they also manipulate children. Most commercials targeted for child-related products are aired on the children's channel or during commercial breaks at a kid's movie. As an adult, you are inclined to indulge your children and find creative ways to celebrate events such as Valentine's Day, which has now become a major commercial event. Marketers prepare for such events weeks ahead.

Beauty pageants, fashion shows, clothing catalogs, and fashion magazines portray perfect-looking models and celebrities who promote models with ideal bodies, especially targeting teenagers, giving them the impression that wealth and success are a by-product of the slim figure. Hence the many cases of anorexia and bulimia among teenagers and young adults, who are in search of the perfect image at the risk of their health. Marketers exhibit people who are perceived to be beautiful or handsome or celebrities to sell products and earn exorbitant profits. They believe anything can be sold if it appeals to the consumer and is considered attractive. Market manipulation is used to sell the image, manipulating those in search of this perceived image.

The entertaining arts, movies, and music is entertainment enjoyed by most people, but the industry and governments use them as a form of distraction that comes under the category of manipulation. The entertainment industry is controlled by a faction of people who employ specific thought-provoking themes with subliminal messages pull at your heartstrings, bring tears to your eyes, or terrify you.

Movies about doomsday settings give people an idea of the possibility of something like this happening in the future; here again, you notice consumerism at its best when people flock to buy survival equipment.

Another form of control is to identify those groups which patronize or support a doomsday theory and keep them busy. Many individuals own a survival bag, packed and ready, in the expectation of such an incident. They have platforms like a YouTube channel to talk about this and encourage others to follow suit.

Military invasions, aliens, and zombie apocalypses are some of the examples that you may have witnessed. People have come together to form groups that theorize on these hypothetical events. Artists, no doubt, make a lot of fame and money in this industry by their work and can influence their fans on subjects that they support. So, they are used as tools to impart these types of ideas. These forms of entertainment mask the true nature of the problems the world is facing.

Nicholas West, in his global research post about Predictive Programming, had this to say; he believes predictive programming is real, although many are still in denial. He invites anyone to examine the series of documentaries prepared by Alan Watt and arrive at any other conclusion. Predictive programming originates chiefly in Hollywood, where the large screen can offer a vast vision of where society is heading. You could examine the books and movies which you thought were science fiction or mind-boggling and compare them with society today. "Vigilant Citizen" is a good resource that will make you rethink what "entertainment" is all about.

Music is one of the many powerful art forms. It can create mental environments full of good and bad feelings. Some songs soothe and bring you happiness. But some song lyrics can be quite destructive or disturbing to hear, and they target the young and susceptible minds. These songs are more like satanic chants. An example would be the Japanese cult leader who used rhythmic chants to hypnotize his subjects and cause a terrorist event in the subway of Japan, releasing serine gas and injuring hundreds of people.

These groups are disguised to look attractive or "cool." Their themes are mostly seasonal, as they change from time to time to suit the situation and audience, taking advantage of huge concerts and music festivals that keep people distracted from their problems. Music can manipulate our emotions and actively engage an audience.

Extensive psychological research has gone into making music designed to control the workers in a factory or business, so they don't recognize the demands being put on them by their employer for the benefit of the company. The tempo of the tune can speed up to increase productivity, and so on. Elevator music, spa music, and lobby music was also created for a similar purpose; to keep you calm and relaxed.

Soundtracks played at movies can also play on your emotions. Can you recall your own experience of sitting in the dimly lit theatre, anticipating what's to come, and then remember hearing a soundtrack that may have attached itself to a memory playing on your emotions? Good or bad, you may leave the cinema feeling enlightened, influenced, or affected.

Social Media

A New Age phenomenon to which almost every adult and youngster is addicted is social media. An overflow of disinformation and propaganda is effortlessly spread. You are monitored through Facebook, Instagram, Twitter, and Tumbler, just to mention a few. Social media has a large market and has become quite an annoying medium utilizing a personal formula where advertising is tailor-made for you. They use the information you provide, such as your likes and comments, pages visited, status updates, etc. to design a perfect approach because they have summed up your preferences with their technology. In this instance, a machine gets to manipulate you.

Be it Google or YouTube, the suggested pages and videos are unending, and the more you watch them the more they tend to give you suggestive topics that can manipulate your thoughts and ideas. You may have started at a certain point, and somewhere down the way after several videos, you don't understand what is happening, and you subconsciously form perceptions and beliefs that weren't part of your conscious mind. There is a certain amount of addiction that takes place where you cannot control the need to get on your devices in order to keep yourself 'busy" with the illusion that it helps you to know the goings-on in your network of people. Most often than not, social media news can be tainted and inaccurate, but occasionally you may find truths in it which you will not find on mainstream media. Various fields of media, including social platforms, can work flawlessly to integrate a general message which would seem to have a ring of truth because it comes from numerous sources simultaneously.

As more governments use it to manipulate public opinion on votes and policies, it is becoming an increasing threat to democracy, according to a new report from the Oxford Internet Institute.

Cults

A cult is a group of people that comes together to perform a ritual or worship, usually revolving around a single leader and his/her ideologies. Some cult practices can be destructive, like the "doomsday cult " that led suicidal murders to take more than 900 lives in Jonestown, Guyana, in 1978. Terrorists are brainwashed to commit suicide missions; psychopaths are brainwashed to commit mass murders.

There is, however, a notable difference between a destructive cult and a non-destructive cult (or religion). Not every harmful cult is particularly religious; many can be motivated by political or financial gains.

In some Asian cultures, we see religious practices that are more ritualistic and ceremonial, and perhaps for some of us, offensive and on the extreme side of fanaticism. They subject themselves to physical trauma to attain a spiritual gain because their leader's doctrine is not questioned.

A cult tends to exploit its members' weakness to gain control over them, often using unprincipled psychological practices to alter thought. You can say that a non-destructive cult tries to improve its members' lives by using spiritual guidance to help them with their vulnerabilities.

Dr. Clark, an assistant clinical professor of psychiatry at the Harvard University Medical School, has in his private practice and with colleagues in Boston, treated and studied more than 500 current and former cult members since 1974. He mentions that in some ways, the damaging effects of cult conversions sum up to a new disease in an age of psychological manipulation because many cult groups have established a similar and quite convincing conversion technique for manipulating the weaknesses of potential candidates. The leaders can influence social and behavioral patterns systematically. They target a specific group like college students or the disruptive youth who have had various kinds of rejections, and here in this group have found acceptance of who they are, giving them a sense of power.

In conclusion, you need to understand how mass mind control is done. It is a fine line between manipulation and brainwashing; you can try to avoid being manipulated, whereas the same cannot be said for the latter. You do know that advertisers are guilty of its use because it's an accepted practice for marketing, and they do openly admit to it. In other areas, the truth is not so obvious. Modern mind control is psychological and technological.

A definite effort is ongoing by those who conduct studies in human psychology and behavior, to catalog and predict human behavior patterns that allow the tyrannical few to control the masses while protecting themselves from the consequences of a fully conscious free humanity. By exposing these methods and opening minds to these exploitative activities, they hope to stand a chance of protecting free will.

Chapter Thirteen: Seductive NLP Language

In this chapter, we will look at some methods of seductive manipulation that can be applied in your daily lives.

All humans are social creatures, and our lives depend on the relationships we create. We thrive on the ability to form successful partnerships. It is in our human nature to attract the opposite sex. Our evolutionary trait is that we are on the constant lookout for a suitable mate. Seduction is the art of charming someone by appealing to their senses, and through the ages, we have come up with many ways to do this. We subconsciously know how to use non-verbal signals to show interest or to see who may respond in kind. Seduction is as old as Adam and Eve. History has given us many examples of how someone has used seduction to their advantage, e.g., Cleopatra enticed both Julius Caesar and Marc Antony, and Lord Byron used his poetry to woo the ladies.

Presently, our modern behavior patterns have become more sophisticated, and though certain old methods are still in use and produce results, it has become a game played by many. By understanding general human behavior patterns and applying them you can become successful at getting the desired results through verbal and non-verbal communication. There are many reasons why seduction can happen. It is not only limited to an attraction of a sexual nature.

A man may want to seduce a female to take her to bed. Seduction can also be used to charm someone, to make him/her feel good about themselves. A woman might want to seduce a wealthy man to have a comfortable financial life. A singer may want to seduce the crowds with her charm to sell her music. A woman can seduce her boss to get a promotion. A con man can seduce a rich lonely old lady to acquire her wealth. Seduction is all around us.

You'd be surprised to know that anyone that tries to seduce another person is attempting a form of mind control, knowingly or not. Be it buying flowers and gifts, wearing perfume, a few flirtatious words, taking someone out and pampering them, seduction has a more profound psychological influence than you may expect, and can be categorized as a form of mind control. We are often trying to discover new ways to coerce someone.

There are plenty of books, websites, and courses on how to seduce a person. While some of these are time-consuming, they may have their merits and work for you. You will discover here that using NLP for seduction is very different from what pick-up artists do. There are no lines or phrases to memorize. It is based on your abilities and skills, and how comfortable you are with its execution.

Techniques in Seduction

1. Positive Language

Selecting your words when you speak to a person is important. Just as a first impression is significant, so are your first words spoken. Words have incredible power over people if used appropriately. You can give compliments or be flirtatious when you know the other person is not feeling offended; making friendly jokes can lighten the mood. You can generally know in which direction the conversation will head by their response to you.

Approaching a person of interest and starting a casual but friendly dialogue that does not indicate any ulterior motive is more likely to help you get to know the person better. Keep your conversation on a neutral topic, making sure you ask for their opinion and make their input important rather than rant on about your own thoughts. You may find a common interest, which will then allow you to continue this topic at a later time and give you a reason to exchange phone numbers if need be.

Perhaps you have an interest in a girl or boy at college; you cannot outright ask for their phone number, but you could start a conversation on a topic that's related to any of the study programs, exchange some ideas, and perhaps offer a book or borrow one. You can now exchange numbers; you have a valid excuse and can build a friendship. You will know after that if you can move ahead or not.

2. Mirroring

It is a valuable skill to be able to subtly mirror the other person's actions and movements, from breathing patterns to voice control, while not making it too apparent. When you and the person with whom you are interacting move in synch and match each other's body language, you are implying that you think alike. He or she will pick up this non-verbal sign automatically, and at the end of the meeting, may feel comfortable to be with you. Typically, we tend to find people attractive if they are more like us. Mirroring can be seductive and can be unconscious.

Copying body language is accomplished by tilting your head, smiling, and/or crossing your legs when they do; looking in the same direction if something has caught their attention, changing your tone to match the other, and running your hand through your hair are other examples.

It is important not to overdo the mirroring and be a copy-cat; anyone can notice that. If he/she dropped a napkin or accidentally broke a glass, you obviously cannot do the same.

3. Anchoring

Anchoring is when an action, stimulation of the senses, or even just a spoken word acts as a trigger for the desired emotion, and the ability exists to recall it again later using that same anchor. Our brains are wired to attach feelings and memories to our senses. It is a cognitive reaction that is unavoidable, and it very much influences our feelings, actions, and decisions.

Positive anchoring can be fun, as it can build up the energy and excitement of interaction and has the potential to build memorable outcomes. It is important that you use techniques to set positive emotional anchors and avoid negative ones. Some of them are:

- Keeping good eye contact, when you share topics of mutual interest or special feelings; it enhances the energy you share.

- Avoiding the bad topics and continuing on the good ones, so that when the other person thinks back to the conversation, it is you they remember.

- Making the other person laugh, bringing in humor that ropes the topics into a personal level.

- Having personal nicknames that are attached to a happy memory.

- Touching the shoulder, hand, or elbow each time you say something to make them feel special.

- Giving gifts that can have sentimental value or act as a memento connected to an event.

It is not just humans that give gifts and try to impress; it takes place in the animal kingdom as well. Some examples are:

1. Male dolphins present a bunch of water weed to the females as part of their courtship behavior.

2. The male haddock courts a female by humming to them.

3. Seabirds bob their heads and flutter their wings to attract a mate.

Humans are much the same. When you need to impress someone, you like to dress up in your best, smell nice, and smile coyly; men like to push out their chests to look strong and heroic. Women like to sway and be more flirtatious in their actions. It is all in the building blocks of our human nature.

Some ways that you can recall these anchoring techniques:

When you hear a specific song, it can bring memories that are attached to it, like your first dance.

Smelling a particular perfume can remind you of someone you cared about.

Looking at gifts can remind you of the happy feeling when you received it.

Seeing flowers can remind you of the moment of receiving it from someone you love, and how you felt at the time of receiving it.

A special book you shared with someone can bring back memories.

If you went shopping and shared an ice-cream and had a good time, then having that ice-cream again can bring back that sensation.

Those same feelings can be recreated by a touch on your shoulder or the holding of hands.

Seeing people with whom you have lost connection is also a trigger and bumping into them after a long time can open a floodgate of a variety of emotions.

The same goes with pain and sadness. Seeing pictures and recalling events shared with a person whom you lost can bring mixed feelings, both sad and happy.

4. Implanted Commands

This is a phrase that is a question or command in the middle of a sentence. It becomes an acceptable suggestion to the unconscious mind. However, the phrases surrounding the command in the sentence will disguise the implanted command so that it goes unnoticed by your target's conscious mind.

(You may refer to detailed techniques from the works of Derek Rake, who is famous for the Shotgun Method.)

Using the word "because" has the effect of imposed authority, which strengthens the Implanted Command on a subconscious mind as it gives the person a reason for consideration.

When you try to order somebody to do something, their self-worth will battle at resisting you, because nobody wants to be bossed around. It is far more effective to give someone the impression that they are not being instructed to do something, but instead being given an option to decide. Everyone prefers to have a choice. You can plant subtle commands in someone's head, which are favorable to you. The suggestion can even be a negative one, like asking someone not to think of them or not to get too attached to something or someone, and sometimes they tend to do exactly that.

5. Fractionation

Fractionation is a dark pattern of using emotion to invoke both pleasure and pain, and if used with malicious intent, can cause harm. Fractionation is a common hypnosis technique used by hypnotherapists to rapidly and effortlessly send their clients into a state of subconsciousness and relaxation. These techniques may be put to use in various environments and situations of seduction. However, they are not for the purpose of using people and playing with their emotions or to victimize them. It is also not a technique that can be used casually; it is used by therapists who are experienced in the fields of hypnotherapy.

It was utilized by Derek Rake for matchmaking and courtship.

Here is how Fractionation works:

You start by making the other person recall a happy or joyous experience. You ask him or her to describe this experience as vividly as they remember it, because the stronger the feeling becomes, the better it is. You then duplicate the same process by making him or her recall an unhappy or distressing experience. Repeat the same, by making him/ her go through an emotional flood with you. At this point is, you are getting the person to feel both sad and happy emotions rapidly while you are in his/her presence and are sharing in the experience of that memory. They will then link those flooding sensations to you, and it will confuse their thoughts into feeling that you have known them for a long time, building trust in you.

The ultimate objective of seducing someone is to help you look friendlier, approachable, and more attractive to the person you're trying to impress. No one single way exists that would work for everyone in every situation. You will have to be watchful on how you attempt these practices. Also, there is no certainty that the person you are trying this on will fall for such attempts. They may also be well versed in these methods and may sense what you are up to. Hence tread with caution on this matter or else you may be spoiling a great opportunity of forming a wonderful relationship.

Chapter Fourteen: Avoiding NLP Mind Control (and Thinking for Yourself)

To lead a successful life, we all need to influence someone at some point in our lives. Influencing someone is a necessary tool for all of us to survive successfully in some way or the other. But how sure are you that you are influencing someone in a good way or bad? One main focus of NLP is the significance that people hold regarding their thoughts, values, and beliefs. Your intention plays a significant role; it is believed that others can sense and feel your intention. They will also understand if you intend to manipulate them in a negative way and are not going to trust you or come to you no matter what amazing skills you possess. On the other hand, if your intentions are nice and clean, this will help you have a better relationship with the person, and they are going to trust you.

Seven Ways to Manipulate

Some of these techniques that you see below are not done consciously; in fact, some of these manipulations are so unconscious that people don't even realize that they are manipulating others.

1. Gas-lighting technique – when an individual tries to persuade you by saying that your behaviors or limits don't have value. An example of this is when you behave in a certain way and your friend tells you "you're being insane,", or, "nobody would ever behave like you". Such statements are used to make your limits invalid. This technique tries to persuade you by making you doubt your validity, beliefs, and limits. Everyone has their limits, values, and beliefs, and no one has the right to change them because they are yours, and only you know how important they are to you.

2. Becoming an outburst creature – during a normal conversation, an individual is suddenly bursting with anger and starts yelling, making for a huge drama. Avoiding these dramas and giving up on boundaries is all this technique is about. For instance, when you want a cup of coffee, and your friend says that coffee isn't good because it contains caffeine. You share your point of view and she makes a dramatic production, raising her voice and saying coffee contains caffeine, which can cause migraines. To avoid a messy drama here, you will likely give up on your cup of coffee.

3. Seizing the issue – this happens by hijacking the issue. They try to change the topic by diverting your mind so that you don't defend your side of the issue. They completely hijack the conversation, and the funny part is that they make you feel like you made a mistake, and you may even end up apologizing to them. Now that you know this, when the person tries to distract you from your issue and brings up another topic, walk away and wait for the next opportunity to talk to them politely.

*4. Giving people conditions or warning*s –this tactic is used most of the time to make you do something that you're not interested in doing. If this happens to you, it's always better to give them a direct answer, especially a "NO" if you're not interested. If you're able to answer directly, then definitely they are going to give you more options, and yes, this has been proved.

5. Enforcing non-existent contracts – this happens when someone does something to or for you when you don't actually ask them to. These individuals have a contract that was not actually made with you, but they come to you in the future asking a favor in return. Because they've done something for you, due to guilt, you do in return.

6. Using identification and personality against you – we humans tend to pick up identities such as, "I am a good person, and if I am going to be a good person, I should help others." When others know of this identification of yours, they put you into a situation where you find it difficult to say no because you feel that not being helpful is a sign of a bad person.

How to Defend Yourself from NLP Mind Control

Neuro-Linguistic Programming was developed to enable control of one's mind to protect it from negative thoughts and even mental illnesses. Still, the dark side of this is that some specific groups of individuals use these techniques to manipulate other's minds negatively. Techniques in mind control can be used in the most constructive ways, as well as in the most destructive ways. Here we are talking about the mind control that is negative, unethical, and destructive.

Who Uses It?

- Abusive husbands
- Abusive wives
- Psychopaths
- Manipulating men
- Manipulating women
- Narcissists
- Selfish individuals

Factors that affect the effectiveness of mind control

- The skills of the influencer
- The manipulative techniques that have been used
- The number of techniques that have been used
- The environment
- The skills of the person to be manipulated
- The voice

How Do You Make Sure that You Aren't Being Manipulated?

1. Keep moving your eyes in random unstable movements – now, when somebody keeps looking at your eyes during a discussion, you will normally feel satisfied because you think that they are paying attention to what you say. But NLP practitioners would keep looking at the movements of your eyes to notice how you access and store data.

2. Be highly cautious about others trying to follow the language of your body – one of the tricks that is done by NLP practitioners is to do the exact same movements as you do. If you are concerned that someone is trying to manipulate you, then you should probably do few more movements to see if the other person is mirroring you.

3. Be attentive of doubtful language – one of the basic strategies that are used by these trainers is that they use a very different and doubtful form of language. This can be a sign of attempting hypnotism.

4. Don't allow yourself to be touched – we all know that it's a common thing when someone touches us, but you need to be conscious of it when someone who is into NLP touches you.

5. Be aware of jargon like "Can you elaborate on it?" and "Can you tell me what exactly you feel?"; these kinds of statements are used during the manipulative process.

6. Be suspicious about permissive language – the best way to make someone do something is to get them into a trance and then give them permission to do it.

7. Don't agree immediately – if you are urged to make a sudden decision, don't do it. Take as much time you want to come up to a decision. It is advised at least to take 24 hours to make the decision. The reason is that right after the discussion, there is more chance for you to make a decision that is favorable to them.

8. Pay attention – notice everything that seems vague to you; NLP trainers have a different way of manipulating than others. Anything that seems doubtful should be avoided. Don't panic and make the situation worse, but slowly get out of the conversation without allowing them to know.

9. Pay attention to what is said between the lines – "A cup of coffee and asleep with me during a winter night is going to be amazing. Wouldn't it be nice?" Obviously, a cup of coffee and a deep sleep during the winter night is definitely amazing, but what is said between the lines? "A cup of coffee and asleep with me...." Pay attention to these statements before agreeing to do so.

10. Trust your instincts – when you feel like somebody is acting weird with you or trying to be different, then you should probably move away. Be capable of spotting things that seem uneasy, different, and not normal.

How to Think for Yourself

Due to the fast-growing world and the rapid development of technologies, it is becoming extremely difficult for us to make choices in life due to all the external influences. Some decisions you make might seem your own but deep inside they might have an influence from somewhere else. The external influences can be negative, positive, or sometimes even neutral, but knowing if this influence exists is in our hands. We also need to think about the extent to which this influence is going to impact our life; is it positive or negative? Is it suitable for me or not?

Now all these questions must be answered by you. Before making choices in life, you need to go slow instead of rushing towards making a decision. Although influences are both positive and negative, we also need to think on our own and make decisions on our own. Because at some point in your life, you will be put into a situation that requires you to think at your best. If you are a person who finds it hard to think on your own, then you might end up becoming a puppet, and others might get a good chance to manipulate you. We all need to agree to the fact that we are all put into cultures and societies where norms, rules, beliefs, and values are already accepted and concluded. We are all compelled and taught to confirm what has already been concluded. Following it up isn't a bad thing, but blindly accepting it without questioning it can make you lack your thinking skills. All the choices we make and all our thinking at some point comes from an influence. You need to be able to hold on to your opinions, examine them, critically evaluate them, and then finally, you should be able to speak them.

Ways to Think on Your Own

a. Have an active sense of self. You need to know yourself better than anyone else; what you like, what you don't like, what you want, and what you don't want. Don't allow others to decide for you.

b. Always be well learned. Examine and cluster information as much as you want before making decisions.

c. Always be adjustable. Look from as many perspectives as you can. Don't think just from your point of view. Look for advantages and disadvantages and be fair in making your decisions.

d. Analyze any possible biases. Are you being fair? Open? And flexible? Sometimes we might hold biases that can bring about a negative outcome.

e. Do not clip yourself to anxiety, regret, guilt, and force. Be strong and build up the courage that you need to stand up for what you believe. Sometimes you might tend to make decisions due to guilt, pressure from the outside world, and fear. Don't ever do this; know your worth and your rights. You are capable of making your own decisions, and you are capable of standing with courage, holding onto what you want.

Advantages of Thinking on Your Own

- It helps you to construct self-confidence and believe in your skills and capabilities

- You gain a higher sense of achievement

- You widen the scope of your mind and advance the power of your brain

- You always become conscious of when others are trying to manipulate you

- Others start respecting you because you stand up for your rights and what you believe

- You are more open to opinions, and you become more flexible

You will not be able to think for yourself if the media and others can divert your mind from your rights. Thinking on your own isn't an easy task. It requires courage, mindfulness, and strength. Neuro-Linguistic Programming is a psychological tool that includes the techniques that are used by successful figures in guiding other individuals to apply these techniques. This approach is about bringing changes in different aspects in an individual's life, like perception, skills for communication, skills for persuasion, and many more. It depends on the different individuals as to how they use this tool. NLP aims to train and produce practitioners who will be able to guide individuals out of their struggles. This tool is only used to make amazing positive changes to help individuals lead their best life.

Conclusion

The next step is to utilize all the useful tools and techniques of NLP in various situations in your life or business and discover how effectively NLP works to create a positive change. You may also try creating your own methodologies or techniques that work best for you.

Be mindful that these techniques aren't scientifically proven but have been tested and developed with experience and results over time.

Each individual is unique in character and behavior, and this is a limitation as to how effectively each technique of NLP could work for them.

Like any other form of therapy, NLP has its pros and cons and should be used carefully with you in control of the process and not having to be dependent on the techniques to find your way.

When you are in control of the techniques, you have an option to choose them wisely depending on where, when, and for whom they are employed rather than permitting them to control your mind and thought process. Persuasion, negotiation, or manipulation cannot follow specific fixed steps or procedures to ensure their success. Instead, it could work differently depending on an assortment of variables like behavioral patterns, attitudes, circumstances, and personalities. Therefore, it is totally in your hands to discover a recipe for NLP techniques that will work successfully for you.

References

https://www.cleverism.com/complete-guide-neuro-linguistic-programming-nlp/

https://www.highspeedtraining.co.uk/hub/neuro-linguistic-programming-beginners-guide/

http://www.nlp.com/what-is-nlp/

https://excellenceassured.com/nlp-training/nlp-certification/reframe#targetText=NLP%20Reframe%20%26%20NLP%20Reframing,where%20the%20meaning%20is%20altered.

https://www.nlp-techniques.org/what-is-nlp/six-step-reframing/

https://www.youtube.com/watch?v=8nUeVmIfUI8

https://inlpcenter.org/nlp-anchoring/

https://www.youtube.com/watch?v=3usTlFwJm8U

https://www.youtube.com/watch?v=sePU3Dywc2c

https://excellenceassured.com/354/build-rapport-and-your-success-nlp

https://www.thecoachingroom.com.au/blog/3-powerful-nlp-techniques-to-create-rapport-fast

https://www.youtube.com/watch?v=6SRMvyyDmkc

https://www.youtube.com/watch?v=dENi7K2lX4U

https://www.youtube.com/watch?v=jXCsU3G-dQk

https://www.youtube.com/watch?v=d6O6gQppQSk

https://nlp-mentor.com/nlp-persuasion-techniques/

https://nlp-mentor.com/persuasion-tactics/

https://excellenceassured.com/1906/nlp-language-technique-for-negotiation

https://www.youtube.com/watch?v=fQkGOQPayx0

https://theplaidzebra.com/the-6-nlp-techniques-that-will-turn-you-into-an-expert-negotiator/

https://www.youtube.com/watch?v=ABaa_XH8ICU

https://www.youtube.com/watch?v=Z5-xNxs9rHk

https://www.youtube.com/watch?v=fsroFwaw5pE

https://www.youtube.com/watch?v=jpVw1B69w_c

https://www.dummies.com/health/mental-health/increase-your-positive-thinking-with-neuro-linguistic-programming/

https://www.youtube.com/watch?v=3uWygq9EWPA

https://www.nlp-secrets.com/nlp-confidence.php

https://www.globalnlptraining.com/blog/nlp-trainer-tips-4-ways-boost-confidence/

http://www.robertsanders.me.uk/3-nlp-techniques-to-reduce-anxiety-right-now/

https://www.youtube.com/watch?v=ld8RgK26oPU

https://www.youtube.com/watch?v=a_OPnmt9Clw

https://www.youtube.com/watch?v=P8P2g-CyRB0

https://erickson.edu/blog/is-nlp-manipulative-part-1

https://www.nlpworld.co.uk/matching-mirroring-nlp-manipulation-nlp-world/

https://www.youtube.com/watch?v=ULudZAi1PAU

https://www.youtube.com/watch?v=D9fA1FquJNw

https://medium.com/the-mission/who-controls-your-consciousness-the-battle-for-your-mind-is-real-d57127c8f7da

https://www.youtube.com/watch?v=j9GXXAtbWl8

https://www.psychologytoday.com/intl/blog/brain-chemistry/201803/the-art-brainwashing

http://www.turismoassociati.it/dblog/articolo.asp?articolo=3820 (see video too)

https://listverse.com/2016/04/29/top-10-brainwashing-and-mind-control-techniques/

https://www.cultwatch.com/howcultswork.html

https://derekrake.com/blog/nlp-seduction-patterns/

https://www.youtube.com/watch?v=53X8xiPVgmY

https://ultraculture.org/blog/2014/01/16/nlp-10-ways-protect-mind-control/

https://www.youtube.com/watch?v=XjGCV2XFbSk

https://www.essentiallifeskills.net/think-for-yourself.html

https://nlp-mentor.com/six-step-reframe/

https://excellenceassured.com/nlp-training/nlp-certification/reframe#targetText=NLP%20Reframe%20%26%20NLP%20Reframing,where%20the%20meaning%20is%20altered.

https://www.nlpworld.co.uk/nlp-glossary/c/content-reframe/

https://www.renewal.ca/nlp20.htm

https://nlp-now.co.uk/nlp-reframing/

https://excellenceassured.com/nlp-training/nlp-certification/pacing-and-leading

https://www.thecoachingroom.com.au/blog/3-powerful-nlp-techniques-to-create-rapport-fast

https://www.nlpworld.co.uk/nlp-glossary/r/rapport/

Printed in Great Britain
by Amazon